成旦红　刘昌胜　主编

百年上大画传

Shanghai University: A Centennial Photobiography

上海大学出版社
·上海·
Shanghai University Press
Shanghai, China

书名中"百年"集于右任校长书法字体,"上大"集钱伟长校长书法字体

In the book title, "百年" (bǎi nián, meaning centennial), calligraphed by President Yu Youren;
"上大"(shàng dà, meaning Shanghai University), calligraphed by President Qian Weichang

本书编委会

主　　　任　　成旦红　刘昌胜
常务副主任　　段　勇
副　主　任　　龚思怡　欧阳华　吴明红　聂　清
　　　　　　　汪小帆　苟燕楠　罗宏杰　忻　平
委　　　员　　（按姓氏笔画为序）
　　　　　　　王远弟　王国建　朱明原　刘长林　刘文光
　　　　　　　刘绍学　许华虎　许　瑞　孙伟平　李　坚
　　　　　　　李明斌　吴仲钢　吴英俊　沈　艺　张元隆
　　　　　　　张文宏　张　洁　张勇安　张基涛　陆　瑾
　　　　　　　陈志宏　竺　剑　金　波　孟祥栋　胡大伟
　　　　　　　胡申生　秦凯丰　顾　莹　徐有威　徐国明
　　　　　　　陶飞亚　曹为民　彭章友　傅玉芳　曾文彪
　　　　　　　曾　军　褚贵忠　谢为群　潘守永　戴骏豪

主　　　编　　成旦红　刘昌胜

执 行 主 编　　段　勇

执行副主编　　曾文彪　胡申生　刘长林

执 行 编 辑　　纪慧梅　谢　瑾　宋亚丽

英 文 翻 译　　曾桂娥　朱音尔　张　颖

从峥嵘岁月里走来，这里描摹着风云激荡中无数青年的奋进之路，且行且歌，与国家民族命运交织，耕耘出一片新天地。在这里，我们品读峥嵘岁月、钩沉光辉历史，感悟"养成建国人才，促进文化事业"的历史足迹，倾听"武有黄埔，文有上大""北有五四时期的北大，南有五卅时期的上大"的历史回响。

从时代大潮中走来，这里收藏着时空坐标下动人心弦的珍贵瞬间，鲜活如初，与城市发展脉搏相连，阅往知今思悟新成长。在这里，我们融入改革开放的洪流，建设中国特色社会主义。呼吸与共中，四校携手并进；伟业流长中，实现教育兴国。日月星辰，时光流转，朝着与上海这座城市齐名的目标奋勇向前。

从新的征程中走来，这里记录着发展变迁中鼓舞人心的铿锵字句，掷地有声，与历史文化一脉相连，代代传承添加新注解。在这里，我们赓续红色基因和改革基因，发扬钱伟长教育思想，沿着校训精神指引的方向，逐梦奔跑，步履不停，以创新追求卓越，以包容聚合力量，在世界大学行列中书写鲜明印记，在践行上海城市品格中彰显上大特质。

抚今追昔，一幅幅画面，一个个人物，一段段往事，串联起百年上大激情澎湃的历史画卷……

Shanghai University (SHU), since her establishment in the 1920s, has gone through a century of changes and challenges with the nation. In her early days, she committed herself to cultivating national leaders and promoting cultural undertakings, which won her a reputation as prestigious as the Huangpu Military Academy (also known as the Whampoa Military Academy), and a recognition as crucial as Peking University to the progressive movements.

Catering to the development needs of the city of Shanghai and the country during the reform and opening-up in the 1980s, Shanghai University was re-founded for the fostering of interdisciplinary and practical talents for the economic and industrial construction. Nearly a decade later, a new Shanghai University was created by merging and consolidating four colleges and universities. Carrying out President Qian Weichang's (also known as Chien Wei-zang) thought on education and keeping abreast with the social needs of quality-higher education, the new Shanghai University has quickened her development pace with the rapid growth of Shanghai City.

In the new era, inspired from "pursuing excellence" and "being the first to share the world's woes and the last to rejoice in its weal" in the school motto, the new Shanghai University has attained noticeable achievements and made steady progress towards a world-class comprehensive university, which recalls and showcases the school's spirit and cultural inheritance of "seeking truth and innovations" passed down during her century-long history, together with the distinctive characteristics of the city of Shanghai.

This centennial photobiography, a narrative of the passionate history of Shanghai University, bears memories of the past, records attainments of the present, and embraces possibilities of a more promising future.

目 录
CONTENTS

第一部分　1922—1927 年的上海大学 / 1
Part I　Shanghai University in 1922-1927

一　青云发轫　校址几迁 / 3
　　Foundation and Relocations

二　红色学府　革命渊薮 / 26
　　A Center for Progressive Thoughts

三　教学名师与演讲名人 / 57
　　Outstanding Professors and Renowned Orators

四　知名学生 / 67
　　Notable Alumni

五　追认学籍　筹划复校 / 75
　　Recognition of Student Status and Re-operation of SHU

附　汪伪时期的"国立上海大学"（1941—1945 年）/ 79
　　Appendix: The Puppet "National Shanghai University" (1941–1945)

第二部分　1958—1994 年的"四校" / 81
Part II　"Four Institutions" in 1958-1994

一　上海工业大学 / 83
　　Shanghai University of Technology (SUT)

二　上海科学技术大学 / 115
　　Shanghai University of Science and Technology (SUST)

三　上海大学 / 145
　　Shanghai University

四　上海科技高等专科学校 / 169
　　Shanghai College of Science and Technology (SCST)

第三部分　1994年至今的上海大学　/　179
Part III　Shanghai University from 1994 to Now

- 一　合并组建　/　181
  Merger and Establishment
- 二　改革与战略发展　/　186
  Reform and Strategic Development
- 三　党的建设　/　200
  Party Building
- 四　教育教学改革　/　207
  Educational Reform
- 五　人才培养　/　220
  Talent Cultivation
- 六　科学研究　/　237
  Scientific Research
- 七　教师队伍　/　268
  Faculty and Staff
- 八　国际交流与合作　/　288
  International Exchanges and Cooperations
- 九　服务社会　/　298
  Social Services
- 十　精神文明建设　/　302
  Campus Activities
- 十一　校友工作　/　313
  Alumni Activities

百年上大，世代情缘　/　319
SHU Memories, Passing Down Generations

第一部分

1922—1927 年的上海大学

1922年10月23日成立的上海大学，是在中国共产党和国民党酝酿合作的背景下，由共产党人主导，与国民党人合作创办的。上海大学克服种种困难，艰难办学，吸引四方热血青年影从云集，在总计不到五年的办学时间里，为中国革命和建设汇聚、培养了一大批杰出人才，在当时就赢得了"武有黄埔，文有上大""北有五四时期的北大，南有五卅时期的上大"的美誉。

Part I

Shanghai University in 1922-1927

Shanghai University was co-founded on October 23, 1922 by members of the Communist Party of China (CPC) and the Kuomintang (KMT) during the early period of the two parties' cooperation. After its establishment, SHU struggled through sorts of difficulties, attracted enthusiastic youths from all over the country, and gradually grew into a renowned center for China's emerging progressive movements. SHU cultivated a large number of outstanding talents for China's revolution and construction, winning a reputation as prestigious as the Huangpu Military Academy (HMA), and recognized as crucial to the May Thirtieth Movement as Peking University to the May Fourth Movement.

一

青云发轫　校址几迁
Foundation and Relocations

　　1922年10月，位于闸北青岛路（后改为青云路）的东南高等专科师范学校因校政腐败被改组，重建定名为上海大学，国民党元老于右任应邀担任校长。

Shanghai University was founded on Qingdao Road (later renamed Qingyun Road), Zhabei, in October 1922. Yu Youren, a veteran KMT member, was appointed President.

（一）学校成立　　Founding of SHU

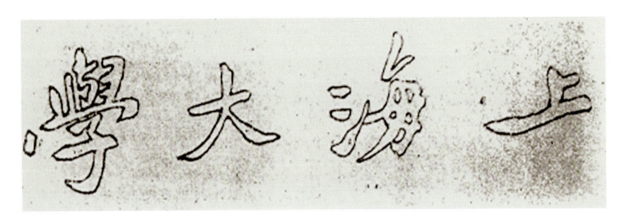

于右任题写的"上海大学"校牌

Shanghai University, inscribed by Yu Youren

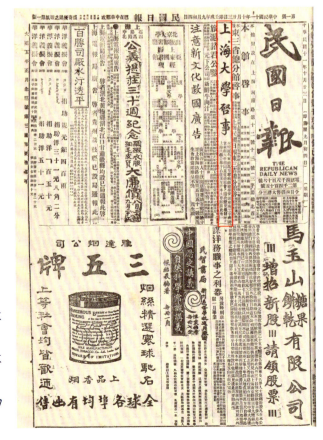

1922年10月23日，《民国日报》头版刊登《上海大学启事》："本校原名东南高等专科师范学校，因东南二字与国立东南大学相同，兹从改组会之议决变更学制，定名上海大学，公举于右任先生为本大学校长。"

"Notice of Shanghai University," published on the front page of *The Republican Daily*, announcing its establishment, October 23, 1922

（二）校址变迁　Relocations of Campuses

1. 青云里校舍　School Buildings in Qingyun Lane

闸北青岛路青云里（今静安区青云路上海市第六十中学）（1922年10月23日—1924年2月）

Qingyun Lane, Qingdao Road, Zhabei (today's Shanghai No. 60 Middle School on Qingyun Road, Jing'an District) (October 23, 1922- February 1924)

上海市第六十中学

Shanghai No. 60 Middle School

上海大学遗址铭牌

Inscription of "Former Site of Shanghai University"

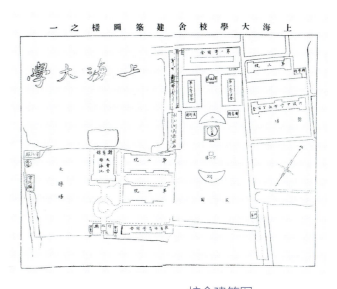

校舍建筑图

Architectural Drawing of SHU

1923年8月12日，学校召开首次评议会，议决在闸北宋园（今闸北公园）建社会科学院、图书馆及学生宿舍。但该方案未能付诸实施。

On August 12, 1923, SHU convened the council and decided to build a social science academy, a library, and student dormitories in Song Yuan (today's Zhabei Park). But the plan failed to be implemented.

1987年11月17日，上海市人民政府将上海大学遗址定为"上海市纪念地点"。

Former Site of Shanghai Uniersity was designated as "Memorial Site under the Protection of Shanghai Municipality" by Shanghai Municipal People's Government on November 17, 1987.

2. 西摩路校舍　School Buildings on Ximo Road

公共租界西摩路29号（今陕西北路南阳路路口）（1924年2月—1925年6月）
No. 29 Ximo Road in the International Settlement (at today's intersection of North Shaanxi Road and Nanyang Road) (February 1924-June 1925)

1959年5月26日，上海市人民委员会将上海大学旧址定为"上海市文物保护单位"。

Former Site of Shanghai University was designated as "Shanghai Culture Relic Protection Site" by Shanghai Municipal People's Committee on May 26, 1959.

上海大学旧址（西摩路）铭牌
Inscription of "Former Site of Shanghai University" (on Ximo Road)

1925年6月4日，学校被公共租界当局巡捕和英国海军陆战队包围，并进行武力搜捕查封。9月7日，北洋政府外交部特派江苏交涉员许沅呈文外交部，详述"上海大学被租界海军搜索发生损失要求赔偿据情陈请汇案"。

A letter was submitted on September 7, 1925 to the Ministry of Foreign Affairs of the Government of the Chinese Republic by Xu Yuan, a special representative in Jiangsu, detailing that "SHU was closed down by the British Marines and the police in the International Settlement, and claimed compensation for the losses."

1925年9月10日，北洋政府外交部总长沈瑞麟在许沅呈送的"上海大学被租界海军搜索发生损失要求赔偿据情陈请汇案"公文上加盖"沈阅"章

The letter submitted by Xu Yuan was read and sealed by Shen Ruilin, Chief of the Ministry of Foreign Affairs on September 10, 1925.

3. 方斜路东安里临时校舍
Temporary School Buildings at Dong'an Lane, Fangxie Road

《申报》1925年6月5日刊登消息，上海大学于西门方浜桥勤业女子师范学校设临时办事处。

Shun Pao reported that SHU set up a temporary office at Qinye Girls' Normal School on June 5, 1925.

《申报》《民国日报》1925年6月8日刊登消息，上海大学租借西门方斜路东安里18号、29号等房屋为临时校舍。

Shun Pao and *The Republican Daily* reported that SHU set up temporary school buildings at No. 18 and No. 29, Dong'an Lane, Fangxie Road on June 8, 1925.

4. 青云路师寿坊临时校舍
Temporary School Buildings in Shishou Lane, Qingyun Road

闸北青云路师寿坊（1925年9月—1927年3月）

Shishou Lane, Qingyun Road, Zhabei (September 1925-March 1927)

5. 江湾校舍　School Buildings in Jiangwan

1927年5月，上海大学被封闭，其后江湾校舍成为国立劳动大学农学院校舍。

After the closure of SHU in May 1927, the Jiangwan campus became the site of Agricultural College of National Labor University.

江湾西镇圣堂路奎照路（1927年4—5月）
Shengtang Road and Kuizhao Road, Jiangwan West Town (April-May 1927)

1932年1月28日，淞沪抗战爆发，日军入侵上海后，上海大学江湾校舍毁于战火。

The school buildings of Jiangwan campus were destroyed by war after the outbreak of the January 28th Wusong-Shanghai Battle of Resistance in 1932.

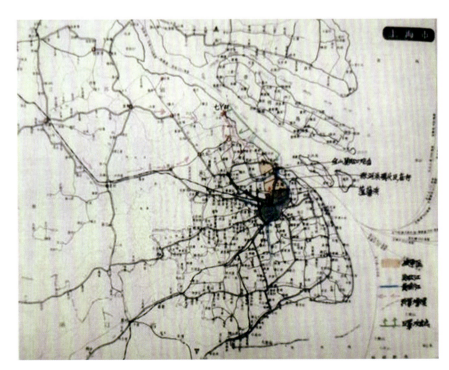

（三）国共两党领导人与上海大学
SHU and the KMT and CPC Leaders

1. 中国国民党领导人　Leaders of the KMT

孙中山（1866—1925），名文，在日本化名中山樵，后遂以中山名。广东香山（今中山）人。中国近代伟大的民主革命家。1923年9月，应上海大学评议会之邀，担任上海大学名誉校董。曾两次作出批示，指示上海大学接受因参加反对军阀和贿选而遭到安徽当局通缉的爱国学生进入上海大学学习。还应上海大学学生社团孤星社请求，为《孤星》旬刊题写刊名。

Sun Yat-sen (1866-1925) was a great democratic revolutionist in modern China. In September 1923, Sun was invited to serve as Honorary Board Director of SHU. At the request of Neptune, a student association of SHU, he inscribed the title for the journal *Neptune*.

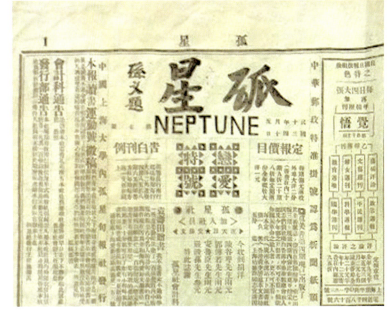

孙中山为《孤星》旬刊题写的刊名
The title of *Neptune* inscribed by Sun Yat-sen

廖仲恺（1877—1925），广东归善（今惠州）人。中国民主革命家。1905年加入同盟会，1923年后协助孙中山改组国民党，任国民党中央执行委员会常委。1924年10月29日，安徽逃亡学生皮言智等上书孙中山要求进入上海大学学习，孙中山将来信下发国民党中执会第五十八次会议讨论通过，由廖仲恺代表中执会将会议讨论结果转上海大学办理。

Liao Zhongkai (1877-1925), a Chinese democratic revolutionist, joined the Tongmenghui (Chinese Revolutionary League) in 1905, helped Sun Yat-sen reorganize the KMT after 1923, and served as a member of the Standing Committee of the Central Executive Committee of the KMT. On October 29, 1924, Pi Yanzhi, a progressive student from Anhui, requested to enter SHU in his letter to Sun Yat-sen. Sun sent a letter to the 58th meeting of the KMT Central Executive Committee for discussion and approval. Liao, on behalf of the committee, informed SHU of the results of the meeting.

2. 中国共产党领导人　Leaders of the CPC

陈独秀（1879—1942），字仲甫，安徽怀宁十里铺（今属安庆）人。中国共产党的创始人和早期领导人。上海大学成立以后，写给陈望道一张署名"知名"的条子，上写："上大请你组织，你要什么同志请开出来，请你负责。"1924年10月10日在国民党右派制造的"黄仁事件"以后，发表文章，强烈谴责国民党右派打死打伤上海大学黄仁等学生的暴行。

Chen Duxiu (1879-1942) was a founder and early leader of the CPC. After the establishment of SHU, he wrote a note to Chen Wangdao, expressing his full support for the running of SHU. After the Huang Ren Incident triggered by the rightists of the KMT on October 10, 1924, Chen strongly condemned the deaths and injuries of SHU students caused by the KMT rightists.

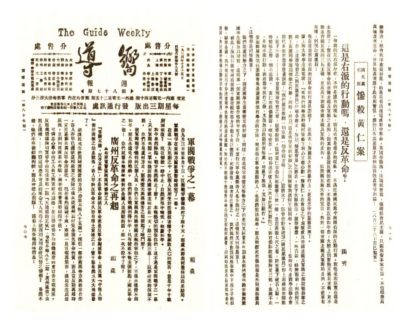

在《向导》周报1924年第87期"国民党右派惨杀黄仁案"专栏上，陈独秀以笔名"独秀"发表题为《这是右派的行动吗，还是反革命？》的文章

Chen Duxiu published an article entitled "Is This a Rightist Action or a Counter-Revolution?", criticizing the KMT for the Huang Ren Incident on *The Guide Weekly*, 1924.

百年上大 画传

李大钊（1889—1927），字守常，直隶乐亭（今属河北）人。中国无产阶级革命家，中国最早的马克思主义者，中国共产党的创始人和早期领导人。上海大学成立后，向于右任推荐了邓中夏、瞿秋白等中国共产党人到上海大学任职任教，并四次到上海大学发表演讲——"演化与进步""社会主义释""史学概论""劳动问题概论"。

Li Dazhao (1889-1927) was a proletarian revolutionist, founder, and early leader of the CPC. After the establishment of SHU, Li recommended Deng Zhongxia, Qu Qiubai, and other Communists to Yu Youren to teach at SHU, and delivered four lectures at SHU on "Evolution and Progress," "Interpretation of Socialism," "Introduction to Historiography," and "Introduction to Labor Issues."

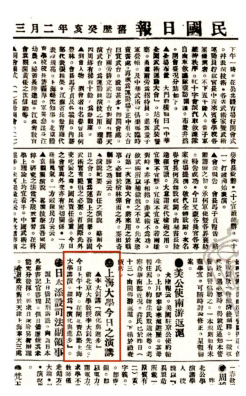

1923年4月15日，《申报》报道：《李大钊今晨在上海大学演说》
The news "Li Dazhao Will Lecture at SHU This Morning," reported by *Shun Pao*, April 15, 1923

1923年4月15日，《民国日报》报道：《上海大学今日之演讲·李大钊讲"演化与进步"》
The news "Lecture at SHU Today: Evolution and Progress by Li Dazhao," reported by *The Republican Daily*, April 15, 1923

中共中央文献研究室编《毛泽东年谱（一八九三—一九四九 上卷）》，中央文献出版社 2013 年版，第 122 页

The Chronicle of Mao Zedong (1893-1949). Beijing: Central Party Literature Press, 2013, vol. 1, p.122

中共中央文献研究室编《毛泽东年谱（一八九三—一九四九 中卷）》，中央文献出版社 2013 年版，第 116 页

The Chronicle of Mao Zedong (1893-1949). Beijing: Central Party Literature Press, 2013, vol. 2, p.116

  1924 年 3 月 20 日，毛泽东出席国民党上海执行部第四次执行委员会会议，并作记录。会议讨论在上海大学设立"现代政治班"问题。1926 年 5 月 7 日，国民党中央执委会常务委员会召开第二十六次会议，毛泽东出席会议。会议决定："命令财政部，关于上海大学补助费案，无论财政如何困难，务须依照第一次全国代表大会决议，每月津贴千元；在财政部未给领以前，暂由中央宣传费项下挪借。"当时国民党中央宣传部代部长为毛泽东。1939 年 3 月 4 日，毛泽东出席中共中央书记处会议，会议讨论陕北公学和职工学校的方针。毛泽东在发言中指出："陕北公学是统一战线性质的学校，像过去的上海大学。"

  On March 20, 1924, Mao Zedong attended the fourth Executive Committee Meeting of the KMT Executive Department in Shanghai, discussing the establishment of the "Modern Politics Class" at SHU. On May 7, 1926, Mao attended the 26th meeting of the Standing Committee of the Central Executive Committee of the KMT, where it was decided that the Central Publicity Department should pay the subsidy to SHU. At that time, Mao served as Acting Minister of the KMT's Central Publicity Department. At the meeting of Secretariat of the CPC Central Committee on March 4, 1939, when discussing about guidelines of Shaanbei Public School and staff schools, Mao remarked: "Shaanbei Public School is united-front type of college, just like Shanghai University in the past."

（四）学校领导
Leaders of SHU

1. 校长、代理校长与其他校行政领导　President, Acting President and Other Administrative Leaders

于右任（1879—1964），陕西泾阳人，生于三原。1922年10月任上海大学校长。1928年起任国民党中央执行委员会常委、国民政府审计院院长和监察院院长等职。1949年去台湾，1964年11月在台北病逝。

Yu Youren (1879-1964), President of SHU, had served as a member of the Standing Committee of the Central Executive Committee of the KMT, Auditor-General of the National Government, and Supervisory Director since 1928.

校长于右任（1922年10月23日—1927年5月）
Yu Youren, President of SHU (October 23, 1922-May 1927)

第一部分　1922—1927 年的上海大学　　　　　　　　　　　　　　　　　　一、青云发轫　校址几迁

邵力子（1882—1967），浙江绍兴人。上海共产主义小组成员。1922 年 10 月任上海大学副校长。1925 年赴广州任黄埔军校秘书长兼政治部副主任。1927 年后任国民党宣传部部长、国民参政会秘书长等职。新中国成立后，任全国人大常委会委员等职。1967 年病逝于北京。

Shao Lizi (1882-1967), a member of Shanghai Communist Group, was appointed Vice President of SHU in October 1922. Shao left SHU in 1925 and went to Guangzhou to serve as Secretary-General of HMA and Deputy Director of the Political Department at HMA. After the founding of the PRC, he served as a member of the Standing Committee of the National People's Congress, etc.

副校长、代理校长邵力子（1922 年 10 月 23 日—1925 年 5 月）
Shao Lizi, Vice President and Acting President (October 23, 1922-May 1925)

陈望道（1891—1977），浙江义乌人。教育家，语言学家。上海共产主义小组成员。1920 年 8 月翻译出版《共产党宣言》中文全译本。1923 年夏到上海大学任教，担任中国文学系主任。五卅运动后兼任代理校务主任，主持行政和教务工作，直到 1927 年 5 月辞去上海大学教职，是在上海大学任职时间最长的重要领导人。

Chen Wangdao (1891-1977) was an educator, linguist, and member of Shanghai Communist Group. In August 1920, he translated *The Communist Manifesto* into Chinese and got it published. In the summer of 1923, he taught at SHU and served as Chair of the Chinese Literature Department. After the May Thirtieth Movement, he also served as Acting Director of University Affairs, presiding over administrative and academic affairs. In May 1927, he resigned from SHU.

代理校务主任陈望道（1925 年 5 月—1927 年 5 月）
Chen Wangdao, Acting Director of University Affairs (May 1925-May 1927)

陈望道翻译的《共产党宣言》（1920 年 9 月第二版）书影
The second edition of the Chinese version of *The Communist Manifesto* translated by Chen Wangdao, published in September 1920

总务长邓中夏
（1923年4月—1924年9月）
Deng Zhongxia, Dean of General Affairs
(April 1923-September 1924)

邓中夏（1894—1933），湖南宜章人。无产阶级革命家，中国早期工人运动领导人。1923年4月任上海大学总务长。1927年后任中共湘鄂西特委书记、中国工农红军第二军团政治委员等职。1933年被国民党当局杀害于南京雨花台。

Deng Zhongxia (1894-1933), Dean of General Affairs of SHU, was a proletarian revolutionist and leader of the early workers' movements.

校务长刘含初
（1924年10月—1925年2月）
Liu Hanchu, Dean of University Affairs
(October 1924-February 1925)

刘含初（1895—1927），陕西黄陵人。毕业于北京大学，1923年初到上海大学任教，1924年10月任校务长。1925年2月离开上海大学赴西北从事革命活动。1927年8月牺牲。

Liu Hanchu (1895-1927) became a professor of SHU in early 1923 and served as Dean of University Affairs in October 1924.

总务主任韩觉民
（1925年2月—1926年4月）
Han Juemin, Dean of University Affairs
(February 1925-April 1926)

韩觉民（生卒年不详），湖北黄安人。北京大学毕业，理学士。1923年秋到上海大学任教，1925年2月任总务主任。

Han Juemin (dates of birth and death unknown) started to work at SHU in 1923 and served as Dean of University Affairs in February 1925.

教务长叶楚伧
（1922年10月23日—1923年7月）
Ye Chucang, Provost
(October 23, 1922-July 1923)

叶楚伧（1887—1946），江苏吴县人。1922年10月任上海大学教务长，1922年10月至1923年3月兼任中国文学系主任。1927年后任国民党中央宣传部部长、江苏省政府主席等职。

Ye Chucang (1887-1946) was Provost and Chair of the Chinese Literature Department of SHU from October 1922 to March 1923. After 1927, he served as Minister of the KMT's Central Publicity Department, Chairman of Jiangsu Provincial Government, etc.

教务长瞿秋白
（1923年7—12月）
Qu Qiubai, Provost
(July-December 1923)

瞿秋白（1899—1935），江苏常州人。无产阶级革命家，中国共产党早期主要领导人之一。1923年7月任上海大学教务长，1923年6月至1924年10月兼任社会学系主任。1927年八七会议以后，任中共中央临时政治局常委并主持中央工作。1934年在中央苏区任中华苏维埃共和国教育人民委员、苏维埃大学校长。1935年6月18日在长汀就义。

Qu Qiubai (1899-1935) was a proletarian revolutionist and early leader of the CPC. He served as Provost of SHU in July 1923. From June 1923 to October 1924, he also served as Chair of the Sociology Department. After the August Seventh Meeting in 1927, he was elected a member of the Standing Committee of the Provisional Political Bureau of the CPC Central Committee and presided over the work of the Central Committee.

学务长何世桢
（1923年12月—1924年10月）
He Shizhen, Dean of Student Affairs
(December 1923-October 1924)

何世桢（1895—1972），安徽望江人。1922年获美国密歇根大学法学博士学位。1923年12月任上海大学学务长，1923年秋至1924年12月兼任英国文学系主任。上海持志大学创办人。1972年病逝于上海。

He Shizhen (1895-1972) obtained a doctor's degree in law from the University of Michigan in 1922. He served as Dean of Student Affairs of SHU in December 1923 and served as Chair of the English Department from autumn 1923 to December 1924.

正、副校长与其他校行政领导一览

President, Vice President and Other Administrative Leaders

职　务	姓　名	任职时间
校长	于右任	1922 年 10 月 23 日—1927 年 5 月
副校长、代理校长	邵力子	1922 年 10 月 23 日—1925 年 5 月
代理校务主任	陈望道	1925 年 5 月—1927 年 5 月
总务长	邓中夏	1923 年 4 月—1924 年 9 月
校务长	刘含初	1924 年 10 月—1925 年 2 月
总务主任 （1925 年 2 月，经校行政委员会决定，校务长改称总务主任）	韩觉民	1925 年 2 月—1926 年 4 月
教务长	叶楚伧	1922 年 10 月 23 日—1923 年 7 月
教务长	瞿秋白	1923 年 7—12 月
学务长	何世桢	1923 年 12 月—1924 年 10 月
学务长	陈望道	1925 年 4 月—1927 年 4 月

2. 各系、科、部门行政领导　Heads of Departments and Divisions

文学科主任张君谋
（1923 年 3—8 月）
Zhang Junmou, Chair of the Literature Department
(March-August 1923)

张君谋（1894—1958），名乃燕，字君谋，浙江南浔人。1919 年获日内瓦大学理学博士学位。1923 年 3 月任上海大学文学科主任。

Zhang Junmou (1894-1958) obtained a doctor's degree in science from the University of Geneva in 1919 and served as Chair of the Literature Department of SHU in 1923.

社会学系主任施存统
（1924年10月—1926年4月）
Shi Cuntong, Chair of the Sociology Department
(October 1924-April 1926)

施存统（1899—1970），又名施复亮，浙江金华人。上海共产主义小组成员。曾留学日本。1923年秋到上海大学任教，1924年10月任社会学系主任。1926年4月离开上海大学到广州黄埔军校任教。新中国成立后曾任劳动部副部长等职。

Shi Cuntong (1899-1970), a member of Shanghai Communist Group, entered SHU in 1923 and served as Chair of the Sociology Department in October 1924.

社会学系主任李季
（1926年4月—1927年5月）
Li Ji, Chair of the Sociology Department
(April 1926-May 1927)

李季（1892—1967），湖南平江人。1920年参与筹建上海共产主义小组。1925年到上海大学任教，1926年4月任社会学系主任。译有《通俗资本论》等。新中国成立后，任国家出版总署特约翻译，译有《马克思恩格斯通讯集》《现代资本主义》等，著有《马克思传》等。

Li Ji (1892-1967) became a professor of SHU in 1925 and served as Chair of the Sociology Department in April 1926. He participated in the preparation for the founding of Shanghai Communist Group in 1920, translated many important works, including *A Popular Version of Capital Theory* and *Selected Letters Between Marx and Engels*, and authored *Marx's Biography*.

英国文学系主任周越然
（1925年2月—1926年8月）
Zhou Yueran, Chair of the English Literature Department
(February 1925-August 1926)

周越然（1885—1962），浙江吴兴人。上海广方言馆毕业。1925年2月任上海大学英国文学系主任。新中国成立后，在上海水产学院任教。

Zhou Yueran (1885-1962) graduated from Shanghai Institute of Various Languages and served as Chair of the English Literature Department of SHU in February 1925.

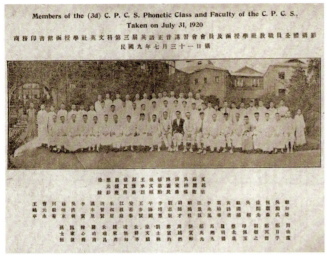

英国文学系主任周由廑（前排右一）
（1926年8月—1927年5月）
Zhou Youjin, Chair of the English Literature Department (first from right in the front row) (August 1926-May 1927)

周由廑（生卒年不详），浙江吴兴人。周越然兄长。1926年8月继周越然任上海大学英国文学系主任。

Zhou Youjin (dates of birth and death unknown), Zhou Yueran's elder brother, served as Chair of the English Literature Department of SHU in August 1926.

美术科主任洪野（肖像）
（1922年10月—1927年5月）
Hong Ye, Chair of the Fine Arts Department (portrait)
(October 1922-May 1927)

洪野（1886—1932），又名禹仇，安徽歙县人。为潘玉良的绘画启蒙老师。1922年任上海东南高等专科师范学校美术科主任。上海大学成立后，续任美术科主任。

Hong Ye (1886-1932), from whom Pan Yuliang started learning western painting, served as Chair of the Fine Arts Department of Shanghai Southeast Normal College in 1922 and continued to serve as Chair of the Fine Arts department after the founding of SHU.

中学部主任兼图书室主任陈德徵
（1923年3月—1924年1月）
Chen Dezheng, Chair of the Middle School Division and Library Director
(March 1923-January 1924)

陈德徵（1899—1951），浙江浦江人。1923年3月任上海大学中学科（后为中学部）主任兼图书室主任。1923年8月7日在《民国日报》副刊《觉悟》发表《发展中的上海大学中学部》。1924年1月辞去中学部主任职务。

Chen Dezheng (1899-1951) served as Chair of the Middle School Division and Library Director of SHU from March 1923 to January 1924.

中学部主任杨明轩
（1924年1月—1925年3月）
Yang Mingxuan, Chair of the Middle School Division
(January 1924-March 1925)

杨明轩（1891—1967），原名荃骏，字明轩，陕西户县（今西安鄠邑区）人。1924年1月任上海大学中学部主任。新中国成立后，任中国民主同盟中央委员会主席、全国人大常委会副委员长。

Yang Mingxuan (1891-1967) served as Chair of the Middle School Division of SHU in January 1924. After the founding of the PRC, he served as Vice Chairman of the Standing Committee of the National People's Congress.

中学部主任刘薰宇
（1925年3—8月）
Liu Xunyu, Chair of the Middle School Division
(March-August 1925)

刘薰宇（1896—1967），贵州贵阳人。北京高等师范学校毕业。1925年3月任上海大学中学部主任。新中国成立后，任人民教育出版社副总编辑。

Liu Xunyu (1896-1967) served as Chair of the Middle School Division of SHU in March 1925 after the graduation from Beijing Normal College. After the founding of the PRC, he served as Deputy Chief Editor of People's Education Press.

中学部主任侯绍裘
（1925年8月—1927年4月）
Hou Shaoqiu, Chair of the Middle School Division
(August 1925-April 1927)

侯绍裘（1896—1927），江苏松江（今属上海）人。毕业于上海南洋公学（今上海交通大学）。1925年8月任上海大学中学部主任。1927年4月被国民党当局杀害。

Hou Shaoqiu (1896-1927) graduated from Shanghai Nanyang Public School (today's Shanghai Jiao Tong University). He served as Chair of the Middle School Division of SHU from August 1925 to April 1927.

中学部代理主任张作人
（1927年4—5月）
Zhang Zuoren, Acting Chair of the Middle School Division
(April-May 1927)

张作人（1900—1991），江苏泰兴人。北京高等师范学校毕业。1924年到上海大学任教，1927年4月任中学部代理主任。新中国成立后，先后担任同济大学、华东师范大学教授。

Zhang Zuoren (1900-1991), became a professor of SHU in 1924 after the graduation from Beijing Normal College and served as Acting Chair of the Middle School Division of SHU in April 1927.

各系、科、部行政领导一览
Heads of Departments and Divisions

职务	姓名	任职时间
中国文学系主任（文学科主任）	叶楚伧	1922年10月—1923年3月
	张君谋	1923年3—8月
	陈望道	1923年8月—1927年5月
社会学系主任	瞿秋白	1923年6月—1924年10月
	施存统	1924年10月—1926年4月
	李季	1926年4月—1927年5月
英国文学系主任	何世桢	1923年秋—1924年12月
	周越然	1925年2月—1926年8月
	周由廑	1926年8月—1927年5月
美术科主任	洪野	1922年10月—1927年5月
中学部主任（中学科主任）	陈德徵	1923年3月—1924年1月
	杨明轩	1924年1月—1925年3月
	刘薰宇	1925年3—8月
	侯绍裘	1925年8月—1927年4月
中学部代理主任	张作人	1927年4—5月

（五）《上海大学章程》制定和《上海大学一览》出版，标志着办学步入正轨
Formulation of *Constitution of Shanghai University* and Publication of *Survey of Shanghai University*, Landmarks for the Development of SHU

1.《上海大学章程》 *Constitution of Shanghai University*

《上海大学章程》于1923年12月由邓中夏主持制定完成，并于当月5日由校评议会通过。

Constitution of Shanghai University was drafted and completed by Deng Zhongxia and approved by Shanghai University Council on December 5, 1923.

《上海大学章程》明确提出上海大学办学宗旨为："养成建国人才，促进文化事业。"

Constitution of Shanghai University stated clearly that the objective of SHU was to cultivate national leaders and promote cultural undertakings.

2.《上海大学一览》 *Survey of Shanghai University*

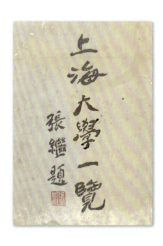

《上海大学一览》于1924年4月出版。封面由国民党元老张继题写。

Survey of Shanghai University was published in April 1924. The title was inscribed by Zhang Ji, a veteran KMT member.

张继（1882—1947），字溥泉，河北沧县人。国民党元老。1923年4月1日，在上海大学作"个人与社会"演讲。1947年12月在南京病逝。

Zhang Ji (1882-1947), a veteran KMT member, gave a lecture on "Individual and Society" at SHU on April 1, 1923.

3. 教职员合影、毕业典礼留影、学生成绩单与毕业证书　Photos, Transcripts and Certificates

1924年6月，全体教职员合影
Staff photo of SHU, June 1924

前排左起：洪野（1）、陈抱一（2）、陈望道（3）、杨明轩（6）、刘大白（7）、于右任（8）、邵力子（10）、何世桢（13）、邓中夏（16）
中排左起：陈铁庵（3）、李瑞峰（5）、瞿秋白（8）
后排左起：许德良（1）、周建人（2）、沈雁冰（3）、田汉（7）、施存统（8）、韩觉民（9）、向浒（10）、翁吉云（11）、
　　　　　邱清泉（12）

1923年7月，美术科第一届毕业生留影
Graduation photo of the first graduates of the Fine Arts Department at SHU, July 1923

第一部分　1922—1927 年的上海大学　　　　　　　　　　　　　　　一、青云发轫　校址几迁

1926 年 7 月 1 日，中国文学系、英国文学系丙寅级举行毕业典礼（中坐长髯者为校长于右任）
Graduation photo of the 1926 Class of the Chinese Literature Department and the English Literature Department, July 1, 1926 (President Yu Youren, the one with long beard in the middle)

学生成绩单和毕业证书
SHU students' transcripts and graduation certificates

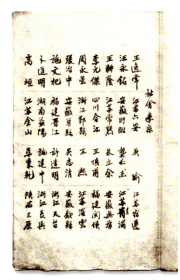

《上海大学学生职员名单》为 1927 年 5 月上海大学被封闭后，由当时上海大学学生手抄。
The list of faculty and students of SHU was written by the students of SHU after the closure of the university in May 1927.

社会学系学生职员名单（局部）
The list of faculty and students of the Sociology Department of SHU (partial)

二

红色学府　革命渊薮
A Center for Progressive Thoughts

　　中国共产党在上海大学积极宣传和传播马克思列宁主义，加强党的基层组织建设，发展了大批优秀学生入党，指示和领导了师生中的党员到全国各地帮助建立党的基层组织，广泛开展反帝爱国斗争，积极投身轰轰烈烈的大革命运动，使上海大学成为国共合作时期一所充满革命激情的高等学府。

The Communist Party of China at SHU devoted itself to spreading and popularizing Marxism-Leninism at SHU, helping establish the Party's grassroots organizations throughout the country, and actively participating in the anti-imperialist patriotic struggles. SHU gradually evolved into a reputed progressive institution of higher education during the cooperation period between the CPC and the KMT, a center for enthusiastic and passionate progressists and revolutionists.

（一）宣传和传播马克思列宁主义
Spreading and Popularizing Marxism-Leninism

一批中国共产党早期党员、马克思主义者在上海大学任教期间，充分利用课堂和党的刊物，结合中国革命实际，发表了大量文章，传播、普及马克思列宁主义，使上海大学成为宣传和传播马克思列宁主义的重要阵地。

While teaching at SHU, the early members of the CPC and Marxists introduced and spread Marxism-Leninism in the classes and published a large number of articles, making SHU a center for progressive thoughts.

《前锋》月刊是中国共产党的机关刊物，于1923年7月1日创刊。由已在上海大学任校务长和社会学系主任的瞿秋白担任主编。

Vanguard, the monthly official journal of the CPC, was founded on July 1, 1923. Qu Qiubai, Chair of the Sociology Department and Provost of SHU, served as Chief Editor.

《向导》周报是中国共产党创办的第一张公开发行的中央机关报。蔡和森是《向导》周报的首任主编，也是主要撰稿人之一；彭述之、瞿秋白、张太雷、郑超麟等上海大学教师也是《向导》周报的主要撰稿人。

The Guide Weekly was the first official newspaper founded by the CPC. Cai Hesen was the first Chief Editor and one of the major contributors to the newspaper.

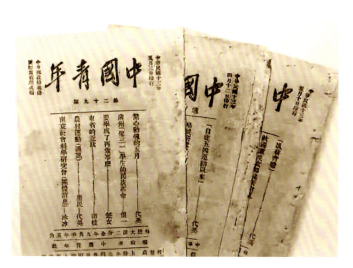

《中国青年》周刊是中国社会主义青年团于1923年10月20日创办的机关刊物，由已在上海大学任教的恽代英担任主编。1925年5月萧楚女到上海大学任教后，协助恽代英编辑《中国青年》。《中国青年》是我国近代史和中国共产主义运动史上最具战斗力和生命力的青年刊物，上海大学教师在刊物上发表了大量文章。

China Youth, a weekly publication, was founded by the Socialist Youth League on October 20, 1923. Yun Daiying was Chief Editor and Xiao Chunü co-edited with him after Xiao became a professor of SHU in May, 1925.

蔡和森（1895—1931），湖南湘乡永丰镇（今属双峰）人。无产阶级革命家，中国共产党的早期领导人。1923年秋到上海大学任教。1925年参加领导五卅运动。中共第二至四届中央执行委员，第五、第六届中央政治局常委。1931年6月被军阀陈济棠杀害。

Cai Hesen (1895-1931) was a professor of SHU in 1923 and an early leader of the CPC. He later became a member of the Excutive Committee of the CPC Central Committee and a member of the Standing Committee of the Political Bureau of the CPC Central Committee.

上海大学丛书之一：蔡和森所著的《社会进化史》
The History of Social Evolution by Cai Hesen

董亦湘（1896—1939），江苏阳湖（今属常州）人。陈云、张闻天的入党介绍人。1924年7月到上海大学任教。1925年10月赴莫斯科中山大学学习。1939年5月受王明宗派活动打击迫害，瘐死苏联远东狱中。1984年平反昭雪，定为革命烈士。

Dong Yixiang (1896-1939), a professor of SHU in 1924, was one of the sponsors of Chen Yun and Zhang Wentian, two of the most important communist leaders of China, when they applied for CPC membership.

1924年3月，上海书店陆续出版《社会科学讲义》1—4集。其中收有上海大学教授瞿秋白的《现代社会学》《社会哲学概论》，安体诚的《现代经济学》，施存统的《社会运动史》《社会思想史》《社会问题》，董亦湘的《唯物史观》《民族革命讲演大纲》等讲义。这些讲义，既是学习社会学、社会哲学的教材，也是马克思主义理论的启蒙读物，在社会上产生了很大影响。

Lectures on Social Sciences (1-4), published by Shanghai Bookstore in March 1924, collect important lecture scripts by a number of professors of SHU, such as Qu Qiubai, An Ticheng, Shi Cuntong, and Dong Yixiang. These scripts are not only textbooks on sociology and social philosophy but also influential reading materials for Marxist theory.

第一部分　1922—1927 年的上海大学　　　　　　　　　　　　　　　　　　　二、红色学府　革命渊薮

瞿秋白所著的《社会科学概论》
Introduction to Social Philosophy by Qu Qiubai

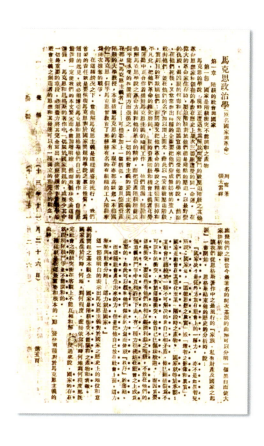

张太雷翻译列宁所著的《国家与革命》第一章，以《马克思政治学》为题，在 1924 年 11 月 26—29 日的《民国日报》副刊《觉悟》上连载。

The first chapter of *The State and Revolution* by Vladimir Lenin, translated by Zhang Tailei, was published with the title "Marx's Politics" on *Enlightenment*, a supplement of *The Republican Daily*, from November 26 to 29, 1924.

张太雷（1898—1927），江苏常州人。无产阶级革命家。1924 年 8 月到上海大学任教。后任中国共产主义青年团中央总书记。八七会议后当选为中共临时中央政治局候补委员。后任中共中央南方局书记兼广东省委书记、广东省军委书记。1927 年 12 月 11 日领导广州起义，任广州苏维埃政府代理主席兼人民陆海军委员。次日在战斗中牺牲。

Zhang Tailei (1898-1927), a professor of SHU in 1924, was later General Secretary of the Communist Youth League of China Central Committee, and elected Secretary of the Southern Bureau of the CPC as well as Secretary of Party Committee and Military Commission of Guangdong Province.

（二）中国共产党最活跃的基层组织，革命的坚强堡垒
An Active Grassroots Organization of the CPC and a Stronghold of Revolution

上海大学集合了一批中国共产党的早期党员和党的领导人，同时又积极在优秀学生中发展党员，因此，上海大学的党员人数一直在全市党员尤其学生党员中占有较大比重。在上海地方党委的基层组织系统中，上海大学党组织以第一党小组、独立支部等形式接受领导，是中国共产党在上海最活跃的基层组织之一，是中国共产党早期革命的坚强堡垒。

SHU attracted a group of early members and leaders of the CPC and developed an array of new members among aspiring students, thus in total accounting for a large proportion in the party members in Shanghai, especially in the student members. The Party organization of SHU, as the first Party Group and Independent Party Branch under the leadership of the Shanghai Party Committee, evolved into the most active grassroots organization of the CPC in Shanghai and a stronghold of the revolution.

1. 中共上海地方兼区执行委员会
Executive Committee of the CPC in Shanghai and Neighboring Districts

中国共产党上海地方兼区执行委员会领导上海市及江苏、浙江两省的工作。1923年7月9日举行第一次会议，决定邓中夏为委员长，沈雁冰为国民运动委员。

The Executive Committee of the CPC in Shanghai and neighboring districts guided the work in Shanghai City, Jiangsu and Zhejiang Provinces. At the first meeting of the committee held on July 9, 1923, Deng Zhongxia was elected Chairman and Shen Yanbing, a member of the Committee of National Movement of the CPC.

沈雁冰（1896—1981），笔名茅盾，浙江桐乡人。毕业于北京大学预科。上海共产主义小组成员。1923年到上海大学任教。新中国成立后，任文化部部长、中国作家协会主席、政协全国委员会副主席等职。

Shen Yanbing (1896-1981), known by the pen name of Mao Dun, a member of Shanghai Communist Group, entered SHU in 1923. After the founding of the PRC, he served as Minister of Culture, Vice President of National Committee of the Chinese People's Political Consultative Conference (CPPCC), etc.

据茅盾晚年回忆：原私立东南高等师范学校借办学牟利，引发风潮，进步学生赶走校长，要我党来接办这学校，"但中央考虑，还是请国民党出面……有利，且筹款也方便些，就告诉原东南高等师范闹风潮的学生，应由他们派代表请于右任出来担任校长，改校名为上海大学。于是于右任就当了上海大学的校长，但只是挂名，实际办事全靠共产党员"。（载《新文学史料》1980年第1期）

Mao Dun recalled in his memoirs that "Yu Youren was only a nominal president of SHU, and it was the CPC members that actually operated the university."

2. 中共上海地方兼区执行委员会第一党小组

No. 1 Party Group of Executive Committee of the CPC in Shanghai and Neighboring Districts

1923年9月27日，中共上海地方兼区执行委员会开会决定，将全市31名党员分成四个小组，第一组10人，为上海大学组，王一知任组长，成员有恽代英、瞿秋白、邓中夏、施存统、向警予、卜士畸等。先后担任第一党小组（即上海大学组）组长的还有林蒸（1923年7月）、许德良（1923年8月）、施存统（1923年9月）、刘剑华（即刘华，1924年1月）等。

At the meeting of the Executive Committee of the CPC in Shanghai and neighboring districts held on September 27, 1923, 31 Party members in Shanghai were divided into four groups, and the SHU group was named the No. 1 Party Group with Wang Yizhi as the group leader.

王一知（1901—1991），湖南芷江人。1923年夏进入上海大学学习。同时在向警予领导的妇女协会工作。读书期间，在《中国青年》等刊物上发表了一系列有关妇女问题的文章。1925年底到广州在邓颖超领导的广州妇女协会担任宣传部主任。新中国成立后，任北京101中学校长。

Wang Yizhi (1901-1991) entered SHU in 1923 and published a series of articles on women's issues.

3. 中共上海大学独立支部
Independent Branch of SHU of the CPC

1926年，中共上海区委批准成立上海大学独立支部，直属上海区委领导。先后担任独立支部书记的有高尔柏、康生。

In 1926, the Independent Branch of SHU of the CPC was approved to be established directly under the leadership of the Shanghai District Committee. Gao Erbai and Kang Sheng successively served as Secretary of the Independent Branch.

高尔柏（1901—1986），江苏青浦（今属上海）人。1924年进入上海大学学习。新中国成立后，任高等教育部第二处副处长。

Gao Erbai (1901-1986) entered SHU in 1924. After the founding of the PRC, he served as Deputy Director of the Second Division of the Ministry of Higher Education.

康生（1898—1975），曾用名赵容，山东诸城人。1925年进入上海大学学习，同年在校加入中国共产党。参加了五卅运动和上海工人第三次武装起义。新中国成立后，任中共中央华东局副书记、山东分局书记、山东省人民政府主席等职。党的八届十一中全会后任中共中央政治局常委、中共中央副主席。1975年12月病死于北京。1980年10月中共中央向全党公布其罪行，决定开除其党籍。

Kang Sheng (1898-1975) entered SHU in 1925 and joined the CPC at SHU in the same year. He participated in the May Thirtieth Movement and the Third Armed Uprising of Shanghai Workers. After the founding of the PRC, he served as Deputy Secretary of the East China Bureau of the CPC Central Committee, and later a member of the Standing Committee of the Political Bureau of the CPC Central Committee and Vice Chairman of the CPC Central Committee.

（三）播撒革命火种，帮助各地建立中国共产党地方基层组织
Spreading Flames of Revolution

上海大学教育教学的一个鲜明特色就是理论联系实际，在这一方面表现最为突出的是要求学生利用寒暑假回到家乡进行革命宣传活动，启发家乡人民的觉悟，播撒革命种子，帮助当地建立中国共产党的地方基层组织。

A distinctive feature of SHU education is to integrate theory with practice.

安徽最早的农村党组织小甸集特别支部的创始人曹蕴真

Cao Yunzhen, founder of the earliest CPC organization in Anhui Province

曹蕴真（1901—1927），安徽寿县人。1923年秋进入上海大学学习。后根据党组织指示，回到家乡开展革命活动，建立了安徽第一个农村党组织"中共寿县小甸集特别支部"，任书记，接受党中央的直接领导。

Cao Yunzhen (1901-1927) entered SHU in 1923 and established the first rural CPC organization in Anhui Province.

湘南党组织的创建者龚际飞

Gong Jifei, founder of the CPC organization in South Hunan

龚际飞（1903—1927），生于湖南湘乡梓门乡（今属双峰）。1923年秋进入上海大学学习。1924年夏受党组织的派遣回到湖南，以《通俗日报》记者的身份参加革命活动，参与创建湘南党组织。1925年10月代表中共衡阳区委对黄克诚进行入党前的谈话。

Gong Jifei (1903-1927) entered SHU in 1923 and participated in the revolution in Hunan.

安徽独山起义的组织者和领导者
方运炽
Fang Yunchi, organizer and leader of the Dushan uprising in Anhui

方运炽（1906—1932），又名方英，安徽寿县人。1923年秋进入上海大学学习。1929年根据党中央指示，以总指挥和党代表的身份成功领导了安徽独山起义，为安徽的武装革命斗争竖起了一面鲜艳的红旗。

Fang Yunchi (1906-1932) entered SHU in 1923 and organized the Dushan uprising in Anhui in 1929.

象山县第一个中国共产党支部成立大会的主持者贺威圣
He Weisheng, host of the inaugural meeting of the first CPC branch in Xiangshan, Zhejiang

贺威圣（1902—1926），浙江象山人。1924年春进入上海大学学习。1924年冬主持了象山县第一个中国共产党支部的成立大会。1926年6月任中共杭州地委书记；同年11月12日英勇就义。

He Weisheng (1902-1926) entered SHU in 1924 and presided over the inaugural meeting of the first CPC branch in Xiangshan.

皖东地区第一位共产党员黄让之
Huang Rangzhi, first communist in East Anhui

黄让之（1902—1934），安徽天长人。1923年进入上海大学学习。为皖东地区第一位共产党员。1924年夏利用暑假回到天长，在家乡点燃了最早的革命火种，为后来天长党团组织的建立奠定了基础。

Huang Rangzhi (1902-1934) entered SHU in 1923. He was the first communist in East Anhui.

建立吉安第一个党组织的罗石冰
Luo Shibing, founder of the first CPC organization in Ji'an, Jiangxi

罗石冰（1896—1931），江西吉安人。1924年2月进入上海大学学习。1926年1月受党中央指派到江西巡视工作，在家乡吉安发展党员，领导建立了吉安第一个党组织中共吉安小组；同年4月任中共江西地委书记。1931年2月英勇就义于上海龙华，是"龙华二十四烈士"之一。

Luo Shibing (1896-1931) entered SHU in 1924. He was among the "24 Longhua Martyrs."

建立沙村第一个中国共产党支部并担任支部书记的沙文求
Sha Wenqiu, founder and Secretary of the first CPC branch in Shacun, Zhejiang

沙文求（1904—1928），浙江鄞县（今属宁波）人。1925年春进入上海大学学习。1926年初回到家乡沙村开展革命活动，成立沙村第一个党支部并任支部书记。1928年8月被敌人杀害于广州红花岗。

Sha Wenqiu (1904-1928) entered SHU in 1925. He led the revolution at Shacun in 1926.

建立六安党的最早基层组织的王绍虞
Wang Shaoyu, founder of the earliest CPC organization in Lu'an, Anhui

王绍虞（1897—1928），安徽六安人。1923年进入上海大学学习。1925年冬回到家乡，组建中共六安特别支部并担任支部书记，这是中国共产党在六安建立的最早的基层组织。1928年4月英勇就义于安庆。

Wang Shaoyu (1897-1928) entered SHU in 1923. He built the earliest CPC organization in Lu'an.

打响琼崖革命第一枪的领导者
王文明
Wang Wenming, leader of the Qiongya Revolution in Hainan

王文明（1894—1930），广东乐会（今海南琼海）人。1924年秋进入上海大学学习。1925年1月赴广州担任"琼崖革命同志大同盟"领导工作。1926年6月在海口市主持召开中共琼崖第一次代表大会，任中共琼崖地方委员会书记。1927年9月23日领导琼崖起义。1930年1月17日病逝于母瑞山根据地。

Wang Wenming (1894-1930) entered SHU in 1924. He organized the Qiongya Revolution.

大革命失败后安徽第一个农民政权的创建者俞昌准
Yu Changzhun, founder of the first peasant regime in Anhui after the failure of the Great Revolution

俞昌准（1907—1928），安徽南陵人。1925年7月进入上海大学中学部学习。1926年夏回到家乡开展党的工作。1928年1月领导成立南芜边区苏维埃政府，这是大革命失败后安徽诞生的第一个农民政权。1928年11月英勇就义于安庆。

Yu Changzhun (1907-1928) entered SHU in 1925. He established the Nanwu Soviet Government in 1928.

中国共产党台湾省地方组织的创建者之一翁泽生
Weng Zesheng, one of the founders of the CPC organization in Taiwan, China

翁泽生（1903—1939），祖籍福建厦门，生于台湾台北。1925年初进入上海大学学习。1926年创立漳州第一个党支部并担任支部书记。1928年4月在上海参与创建中国共产党台湾省地方组织。1939年3月19日病逝于台湾。

Weng Zesheng (1903-1939) entered SHU in 1925. He established the first CPC branch in Zhangzhou and served as its secretary.

（四）开展平民教育工作，深入工人居住区开展工人运动，领导工人罢工斗争
Carrying out Mass Education and Organizing Workers' Strikes

平民教育是国共两党共同开展的一项工作。上海大学在办学过程中，很重视让学生在搞好平民教育的同时，深入工人集中居住的区域，积极投身工人夜校，帮助工人和底层劳苦大众学习文化知识，使他们明白革命道理、提高阶级觉悟。同时也根据党组织的指示，多次领导工人进行罢工斗争。这一系列的工作和斗争，使上海大学的师生经受了考验，提高了能力。

SHU advocated mass education and encouraged students to bring literacy and impart knowledge to laborers and workers. Meanwhile, SHU organized several workers' strikes under the guidance of the CPC.

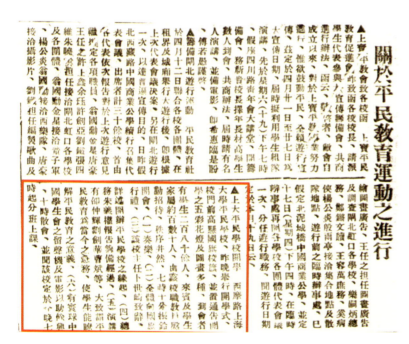

《民国日报》1924年4月16日刊登消息《上大平民学校开学》
The news "SHU Mass School Starts" on *The Republican Daily*, April 16, 1924

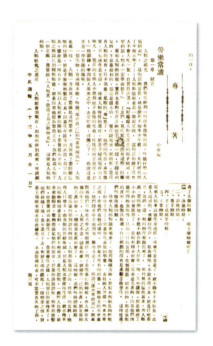

《民国日报》副刊《平民周报》1924年5月31日刊登邓中夏编写的平民学校教材《劳动常识》
"General Knowledge of Labor," teaching material edited by Deng Zhongxia, published by *The Mass Weekly*, a supplement of *The Republican Daily*, May 31, 1924

小沙渡沪西工友俱乐部旧址
Former Site of Xiaoshadu Club for Workers in West Shanghai

平民学校主任卜士畸
Bu Shiji, Director of SHU Mass School

卜士畸（1902—1964），湖南益阳人。1924年4月担任上海大学平民学校主任。1925年春赴广州任黄埔军校代理政治部主任。1964年病逝于台北。

Bu Shiji (1902-1964) became Director of SHU Mass School in April 1924.

平民学校教师张琴秋
Zhang Qinqiu, a teacher at SHU Mass School

张琴秋（1904—1979），浙江桐乡人。1924年春进入上海大学学习。在上海大学平民学校担任音乐教师兼班主任。1925年11月到莫斯科中山大学留学，1931年回国到鄂豫皖苏区工作。后随红四方面军长征，曾任红四方面军总政治部主任。新中国成立后，任纺织部副部长。

Zhang Qinqiu (1904-1979) entered SHU in 1924. She once served as Director of the General Political Department of the Fourth Red Army and later became Vice Minister of Textile after the founding of the PRC.

（五）拥护孙中山，参与国民党工作，批判国民党右派
Supporting Sun Yat-sen, Working with the KMT and Against the KMT Rightists

1924年1月，以国共两党合作为特征的革命统一战线的建立，加速了中国革命的进程，在中国革命历史上出现了轰轰烈烈的大革命。上海大学的党组织和共产党人，认真贯彻和执行中国共产党的统一战线方针政策，拥护孙中山"联俄、联共、扶助农工"的三大政策，参与国民党工作，批判和打击国民党右派。

The Communists at SHU supported Sun Yat-sen and attacked the rightists of the KMT.

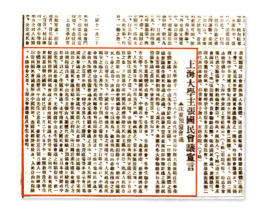

《民国日报》1924年12月3日刊登消息，上海大学发表宣言，拥护孙中山先生关于"召集九团体之预备会议，产生国民会议"的建议
SHU declaring to support Sun Yat-sen's proposal on a national assembly, December 3, 1924

1. 拥护孙中山　Supporting Sun Yat-sen

1924年5月5日，为庆祝孙中山就任非常大总统三周年，国民党上海执行部全体人员在莫里爱路29号（今香山路7号）孙中山寓所举行纪念活动并合影。毛泽东（后排左二）与上海大学教师邓中夏（前排左一）、沈泽民（后排左四）、恽代英（后排右三）、邵力子（后排右二）等出席纪念活动
Some SHU teachers celebrating the anniversary of Sun Yat-sen's inauguration as President of the Cantonese Government, May 5, 1924

1926年纪念孙中山逝世一周年，上海举行盛大集会，上海大学师生出席这次集会
SHU teachers and students attending the parade commemorating Sun Yat-sen's death, 1926

2. 参与国民党上海执行部工作
Participating in the Work of the KMT Executive Department in Shanghai

国民党上海执行部是国民党中央的派出机构，于1924年2月设立，统辖江、浙、皖、赣、沪的国民党党务工作。国民党元老胡汉民、汪精卫、于右任、叶楚伧等分任各部部长，中国共产党人毛泽东、瞿秋白、恽代英、邓中夏、罗章龙、沈泽民、邵力子、张秋人、王荷波、向警予等分别在执行部各部门参加实际工作。

The KMT Executive Department in Shanghai was established in February, 1924. The CPC members and the KMT veterans of SHU worked in different sections of the department.

3. 与国民党右派展开斗争
Fighting Against the Rightists of the KMT

1924年10月10日，上海各界在北河南路（今河南北路）天后宫举行纪念辛亥革命13周年国民大会。全国学生会总代表郭寿华发言时受到国民党右派喻育之、童理璋等的阻挠，上海大学学生黄仁、林钧、何秉彝、郭伯和等上台与喻育之等评理，表示支持郭寿华的发言，即遭大批冲上来的流氓围攻殴打。黄仁被推下高台，当即昏迷，后不治身亡。

Huang Ren, an SHU student, was killed by the rightists of the KMT in the national assembly commemorating the 13th anniversary of the 1911 Revolution at Tianhou Palace, October 10, 1924.

黄仁（1904—1924），四川富顺人。1924年9月进入上海大学学习。10月10日在天后宫举行的纪念辛亥革命13周年国民大会上，遭国民党右派唆使的流氓围攻与殴打致死，成为国共合作时期上海大学最早牺牲的革命青年。

Huang Ren (1904-1924) entered SHU in 1924. He was the first SHU student who sacrificed during the cooperation period of the KMT and the CPC.

4. 广州农民运动讲习所和中央农民运动讲习所
Guangzhou Workshop of Peasant Movement and Central Institute of Peasant Movement

广州农民运动讲习所和中央农民运动讲习所是国共合作时期中国共产党为培养农民运动干部而创办的，其领导和主要教学工作都由共产党人负责。上海大学学生薛卓汉和邓果白分别进入由彭湃任所长主办的第五届农民运动讲习所和由毛泽东主办的中央农民运动讲习所学习。

The Guangzhou Workshop of Peasant Movement and the Central Institute of Peasant Movement were established by the CPC for training peasants cadres. SHU students Xue Zhuohan and Deng Guobai studied in the two Workshops.

薛卓汉（1898—1931），祖籍安徽寿县，生于安庆。1923年秋进入上海大学学习。1925年9月到广州进入由彭湃任所长的第五届农民运动讲习所学习。后至鄂豫皖苏区任中国工农红军第一军政治部副主任。1931年被张国焘以莫须有罪名杀害。

Xue Zhuohan (1898-1931) entered SHU in 1923. He was Deputy Director of the Political Department of the First Army of the Chinese Red Army.

邓果白（1907—1967），安徽萧县人。1925年秋进入上海大学学习。一年后根据党组织安排到武昌参加由毛泽东主办的中央农民运动讲习所学习。新中国成立后在家乡工作。

Deng Guobai (1907-1967) entered SHU in 1925. He studied at the Central Institute of Peasant Movement in Wuchang directed by Mao Zedong in 1926.

（六）"武有黄埔，文有上大"
"SHU, as Prestigious as HMA"

"武有黄埔，文有上大"是大革命时期乃至以后相当长的一个时期社会对上海大学的评价。事实上，黄埔军校和上海大学有着密切的联系，都是大革命时期国共两党培养人才的最重要的基地。

SHU and HMA were the most important talent-training bases during the Great Revolution. The two were closely linked during the revolutionary years.

黄埔军校
Huangpu Military Academy

1. 上海大学学生参加黄埔军校学习　　SHU Students at HMA

张治中（1890—1969），安徽巢县人。1922年冬进入上海大学学习。1923年春赴广州，1925年1月任黄埔军校第三期入伍生代理总队长、军官团团长，1926年任黄埔军校武汉分校教务长。新中国成立后，任民革中央副主席、全国人大常委会副委员长。

Zhang Zhizhong (1890-1969) entered SHU in 1922 and became Provost of HMA Wuhan Branch in 1926. After the founding of the PRC, he served as Vice Chairman of the Revolutionary Committee of the Chinese Kuomintang and Vice Chairman of the Standing Committee of the National People's Congress.

曹渊（1901—1926），安徽寿县人。1923年进入上海大学学习。1924年5月考取黄埔军校，为第一期学员。1926年5月参加北伐，任叶挺独立团一营营长；同年9月1日牺牲于武昌城下。

Cao Yuan (1901-1926) entered SHU in 1923 and was admitted to HMA in 1924.

许继慎（1901—1931），安徽六安人。1923年秋进入上海大学学习。1924年5月考取黄埔军校，为第一期学员。1926年参加北伐，任叶挺独立团二营营长。1930年4月，任中共鄂豫皖特委委员、中国工农红军第一军军长。1931年11月被张国焘下令杀害。1988年被中央军事委员会确定为中国人民解放军军事家。

Xu Jishen (1901-1931) entered SHU in 1923 and was admitted to HMA in 1924.

邱清泉（1902—1949），原名邱青钱，浙江永嘉人。1923年秋进入上海大学学习。1924年7月考取黄埔军校，为第二期学员。抗日战争中，先后参加淞沪会战、南京保卫战、昆仑关战役。淮海战役中任国民党第二兵团司令官，1949年被解放军击毙。

Qiu Qingquan (1902-1949) entered SHU in 1923 and was admitted to HMA in 1924.

季步高（1906—1928），浙江龙泉人。1922年10月进入上海大学学习。1925年6月考取黄埔军校，为第四期学员。1928年1月任中共广州市委书记，同年冬英勇就义于广州红花岗。

Ji Bugao (1906-1928) entered SHU in 1922 and was admitted to HMA in 1925.

李逸民（1904—1982），又名叶书，浙江龙泉人。中华人民共和国开国少将。1922年10月进入上海大学学习。1925年考取黄埔军校，为第四期学员。新中国成立后，任公安部队政治部副主任、军委直属政治部主任、中国人民解放军总政治部文化部部长等职。

Li Yimin (1904-1982) entered SHU in 1922 and was admitted to HMA in 1925.

周大根（1906—1938），又名周秋萍，江苏南汇（今属上海浦东新区）人。1924年进入上海大学学习。1926年考取黄埔军校武汉分校，为第六期学员。1938年12月在率部对日作战中壮烈牺牲。

Zhou Dagen (1906-1938) entered SHU in 1924 and was admitted to HMA Wuhan Branch in 1926.

2. 上海大学师生在黄埔军校任职任教　SHU Teachers and Students at HMA

恽代英（1895—1931），祖籍江苏武进（今属常州），生于湖北武昌。无产阶级革命家，中国共产党早期领导人。1923年夏到上海大学任教。1926年5月任黄埔军校政治主任教官。1927年1月到武汉任中央军事政治学校政治委员，实际负责军校工作。1931年4月被国民党当局杀害于南京。

Yun Daiying (1895-1931), a professor of SHU in 1923 and one of the CPC early leaders, served as a chief instructor of HMA in 1926.

阳翰笙（1902—1993），原名欧阳本义，字继修，四川高县人。1924年秋进入上海大学学习。1926年任黄埔军校政治教官、政治部秘书。新中国成立后，任总理办公室副主任，对外友协副会长，中国文联副主席、党组书记等职。

Yang Hansheng (1902-1993) entered SHU in 1924 and served as a political instructor of HMA in 1926. After the founding of the PRC, he served as Vice Chairman of the Chinese Federation of Literary and Art Circles.

萧楚女（1893—1927），湖北汉阳（今属武汉）人。中国共产党早期理论家。1925年5月到上海大学任教。1926年底任黄埔军校政治教官。1927年4月22日在广州英勇就义。

Xiao Chunü (1893-1927), an early theorist of the CPC and professor of SHU in 1925, served as a political instructor of HMA in 1926.

张秋人（1898—1928），浙江诸暨人。1923年5月到上海大学任教。1926年3月到广州任《政治周报》编辑，后任黄埔军校政治教官。大革命失败后任中共浙江省委书记。1928年2月英勇就义。

Zhang Qiuren (1898-1928), a professor of SHU in 1923, served as a political instructor of HMA in 1926.

高语罕（1888—1948），安徽寿县人。1925年春到上海大学任教。1926年1月任黄埔军校政治教官。1948年4月病逝于南京。

Gao Yuhan (1888-1948), a professor of SHU in 1925, served as a political instructor of HMA in 1926.

安体诚（1896—1927），直隶丰润（今属河北唐山）人。1924年春到上海大学任教。1926年夏任黄埔军校政治教官。1927年5月被国民党当局杀害于上海龙华。

An Ticheng (1896-1927), a professor of SHU in 1924, served as a political instructor of HMA in 1926.

（七）"北有五四时期的北大，南有五卅时期的上大"
"In the North Was Peking University in the May Fourth Movement; in the South Was Shanghai University in the May Thirtieth Movement"

五卅运动是中国共产党领导的一次反帝爱国运动，上海大学师生在党的领导下，积极投身到这股滚滚的革命洪流中，充当了五卅运动的先锋，起到了主力军的作用。所以当时将上海大学在五卅运动中的作用和北大在五四运动中的表现相提并论，称为"北有五四时期的北大，南有五卅时期的上大"。

SHU teachers and students acted as the vanguard and main force in the May Thirtieth Movement.

1. 五卅运动中的先锋　Pioneers in the May Thirtieth Movement

1925 年 5 月 15 日，为抗议日商纱厂资本家撕毁与中国工人达成的协议，顾正红带领工人与日商交涉，遭日商枪击不治身亡。这一事件成为五卅运动的直接导火线。

Gu Zhenghong was shot dead by the Japanese businessmen on May 15, 1925, which triggered the May Thirtieth Movement.

5 月 24 日，在闸北潭子湾广场召开公祭顾正红烈士大会，上海大学学生刘华担任大会总指挥。5 月 28 日晚，中共中央与上海地委召开紧急会议，决定发动群众与学生举行反帝示威，抗议帝国主义列强对中国工人和学生的迫害。5 月 30 日，上海大学、复旦大学、同济大学的 2000 多名学生来到南京路示威演讲、散发传单、高呼口号，租界英国巡捕竟对学生开枪镇压。上海大学学生、共产党员何秉彝等 13 人中枪牺牲，数十人受伤，一百余人被捕，酿成了震惊中外的五卅惨案。

Liu Hua, an SHU student, directed the public memorial assembly for Gu Zhenghong. SHU students attended the protest against the imperialist powers. He Bingyi, an SHU student and communist, was shot dead with the other twelve in the May Thirtieth Massacre.

何秉彝（1902—1925），四川彭县（今彭州）人。1924年初进入上海大学学习。1925年5月30日在南京路参加示威演讲时被英国巡捕开枪打死。

He Bingyi (1902-1925) entered SHU in 1924 and was shot dead in the May Thirtieth Massacre.

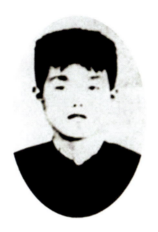

瞿景白（1906—1929），江苏常州人。1923年秋进入上海大学学习。1925年5月30日在南京路参加示威演讲时被租界当局巡捕逮捕；6月11日在公共租界会审公廨的审讯过程中，与会审官和陪审官进行了坚决的斗争，后被无罪释放。

Qu Jingbai (1906-1929) entered SHU in 1923 and was arrested in the May Thirtieth Massacre.

2. 公开成立上海总工会　Establishing Shanghai Federation of Trade Unions

1925年5月31日，上海各工会召开联席会议，一致通过决议，公开成立上海总工会，由李立三任委员长、刘华任副委员长、刘少奇任总务科主任。决定全市总罢工。

The Shanghai Federation of Trade Unions was established on May 31, 1925, with Li Lisan as Chairman, Liu Hua Vice Chairman, and Liu Shaoqi Director of General Affairs.

刘华（1899—1925），原名刘炽荣，字剑华，四川宜宾人。1923年8月进入上海大学中学部学习。1925年2月9日任震惊中外的上海"二月罢工"的前沿总指挥之一，在他的领导下罢工取得全面胜利；5月31日上海总工会成立，担任上海总工会副委员长。1925年12月17日被孙传芳下令秘密杀害。

Liu Hua (1899-1925) entered SHU in 1923 and led the February Strike in Shanghai in 1925.

3. 出版《热血日报》　Founding *Rexue Daily*

五卅惨案发生后，中共中央召开紧急会议，决定出版《热血日报》，由瞿秋白任主编，沈泽民、郑超麟等任编辑。《热血日报》是中国共产党创办的第一张日报，于6月4日创刊。报纸及时传播中共中央的指示精神，及时报道上海和全国人民反帝斗争的消息，无情地揭露帝国主义的血腥罪行和军阀政府的卖国行径，也尖锐地批评党内外对帝国主义实行退让妥协的谬论。报纸出版了24期以后即遭反动当局封禁。

Rexue Daily, the first daily newspaper of the CPC, was founded after the May Thirtieth Massacre to fight against reactionary authorities. Qu Qiubai was the Chief Editor.

沈泽民（1900—1933），浙江桐乡人。1923年底到上海大学任教。1931年3月，任中共鄂豫皖中央分局常委、中共鄂豫皖省委书记。1933年11月病逝于湖北黄安（今红安）。

Shen Zemin (1900-1933), a professor of SHU, led the Hubei-Henan-Anhui Party Committee in 1931.

郑超麟（1901—1998），福建章平人。1925年春到上海大学任教。曾任中央出版局局长。新中国成立后，曾任上海市政协委员。1998年病逝。

Zheng Chaolin (1901-1998), a professor of SHU, served in the CPPCC Shanghai Committee after the founding of the PRC.

（八）参加妇女解放运动
Joining Women's Liberation Movements

向警予（1895—1928），湖南溆浦人。无产阶级革命家，早期妇女运动领导人之一。曾任中共中央妇女部部长、中央妇女运动委员会书记、中央妇女工作委员会委员长。经常到上海大学参加党的会议。上海大学学生钟复光、王一知、杨之华等都直接在她的领导下从事妇女运动。1928年5月在汉口遇害。

Xiang Jingyu (1895-1928) was a proletarian revolutionist and leader of the early women's liberation movements in China. She guided SHU students to join the women's liberation movements.

钟复光（1903—1992），四川江津人。1924年夏进入上海大学学习。在向警予领导下从事妇女运动。1924年12月被推选为上海女界国民会议促成会执行委员。1925年8月任中共上海区委妇女委员会书记。新中国成立后，任全国妇联执委、全国政协委员等职。

Zhong Fuguang (1903-1992), a pioneer in the women's liberation movements, entered SHU in 1924. After the founding of the PRC, she served as a member of the Executive Committee of the All-China Women's Federation, a member of the National Committee of the CPPCC, etc.

杨之华（1901—1973），浙江萧山人。1924年初进入上海大学学习。课余时间，在向警予领导下从事妇女工作，并联络上海大学女生，投身妇女运动，争取妇女解放。1925年10月任中共上海地委妇女部部长、中共中央妇女部部长等职。1945年后在延安任中共中央妇女委员、晋冀鲁豫中央局妇委书记。新中国成立后，任全国妇联副主席、中华全国总工会女工部部长。1973年病逝于北京。

Yang Zhihua (1901-1973), a pioneer in the women's liberation movements, entered SHU in 1924. After the founding of the PRC, she served as Vice Chairman of the All-China Women's Federation and head of the Women's Department of the All-China Federation of Trade Unions.

（九）参加"非基督教运动"
Joining the Anti-Imperialism Movements

1924年8月19日，中国共产党在上海组织"非基督教同盟"，并发表同盟宣言，反对帝国主义的文化侵略。上海大学师生在党组织的领导下，积极投身到非基督教的宣传工作中去。

Led by the CPC, SHU teachers and students actively participated in the Anti-Imperialism movements.

《民国日报》1925年11月8日刊登消息，上海大学非基督教同盟会召开成立大会，饶漱石主持会议。会议推举饶漱石、韩光汉、赵全权、刘汉清、孙金镜五人为执行委员。高语罕、恽代英、杨贤江、萧楚女等上海大学教授在会上发表演讲

The Republican Daily reported the founding of the SHU Anti-Imperialism Alliance on November 8, 1925.

饶漱石（1903—1975），江西临川（今抚州）人。1924年夏秋间进入上海大学学习。新中国成立后，任中共中央华东局第一书记、华东军政委员会主席、中共中央组织部部长等职。1955年3月因"高饶事件"被开除党籍。1975年病逝。

Rao Shushi (1903-1975) entered SHU in 1924 and joined the CPC in 1925. After the founding of the PRC, he served as First Secretary of the East China Bureau of the CPC Central Committee, Chairman of the East China Military and Political Committee, and Minister of the Organization Department of the CPC Central Committee. In March 1955, he was expelled from the Party due to the Gao & Rao Incident.

柯柏年（1904—1985），原名李春蕃，广东潮安（今潮州）人。1924年进入上海大学学习。曾翻译出版列宁《帝国主义论》等马克思列宁主义著作。参加上海大学非基督教同盟会工作。新中国成立后，任驻丹麦王国大使、中国人民外交协会副会长。1985年8月病逝。

Ke Bainian (1904-1985) entered SHU in 1924 and worked for the SHU Anti-Imperialism Alliance.

（十）参加上海工人武装起义，建立上海特别市临时市政府
Joining Armed Uprisings of Shanghai Workers and Establishing Temporary Shanghai Special City Government

1926年7月9日，北伐战争正式打响。上海大学师生为迎接北伐军进军上海，参加了由中国共产党领导的三次工人武装起义，经受了血与火的考验。

SHU teachers and students took part in three armed uprisings of workers in Shanghai in the wake of the Northern Expedition.

1. 积极参加上海工人武装起义
Fighting in Armed Uprisings of Shanghai Workers

杨贤江（1895—1931），浙江慈溪人。中国马克思主义教育理论家。1923年到上海大学任教。1926年底带领学生、工人代表和北伐军联系进军上海的准备事宜。参加了上海工人三次武装起义。1931年7月病逝于日本长崎。

Yang Xianjiang (1895-1931), a professor of SHU in 1923, organized the uprisings and fought in the front.

闸北工人纠察队和上海大学学生纠察队攻占闸北警察署

Workers and SHU students occupying the police station in Zhabei

郭伯和（1900—1927），四川南溪人。1923年进入上海大学学习。1927年3月21日在上海工人第三次武装起义中，率领闸北工人纠察队和上海大学学生纠察队，攻下五区警察署，取得闸北地区武装斗争的胜利。大革命失败以后，任中共江苏省委组织部部长。1927年7月31日就义于龙华刑场。

Guo Bohe (1900-1927) entered SHU in 1923. He organized the armed uprising in Zhabei in 1927.

张崇德（1903—？），浙江临海人。1924年进入上海大学学习。参加了上海工人三次武装起义。1927年9月赴苏联莫斯科中山大学学习。1930年在苏联肃反扩大化时遭秘密逮捕，1937年后屈死于当地。

Zhang Chongde(1903-?) entered SHU in 1924 and joined the three uprisings.

糜文浩（1901—1927），江苏无锡人。1923年春进入上海大学学习。1927年参加上海工人第三次武装起义，负责组织工人纠察队。1927年11月英勇就义于上海枫林桥刑场。

Mi Wenhao (1901-1927) entered SHU in 1923. He worked for the third uprising in 1927.

2. 在上海特别市临时市政府中任职

Serving in Temporary Shanghai Special City Government

1927年3月12日，上海市民代表会议选出上海特别市临时市政府委员19人，其中包括上海大学师生侯绍裘、林钧、何洛3人，林钧兼任秘书长。

On March 12, 1927, the Shanghai Municipal People's Congress elected 19 members of the Temporary Shanghai Special City Government, including three teachers and students from SHU. Lin Jun served as Secretary-General.

林钧（1896—1944），江苏川沙（今属上海浦东新区）人。1924年7月进入上海大学学习。1927年3月22日上海工人第三次武装起义成功以后，成立上海特别市临时市政府，当选为市政府委员兼秘书长。1944年5月被国民党特务秘密杀害。

Lin Jun (1896-1944) entered SHU in 1924. He worked in the Temporary Shanghai Special City Government after the third uprising.

（十一）中国共产党上海大学特别支部和中国共产主义青年团上海大学支部的活动
Special Branches of the CPC and the Communist Youth League at SHU

上海大学师生中的党团员，在任教和求学期间，根据党团组织的指示和安排，参加了全国和上海各级党团组织的领导工作，为开展党团活动和发展壮大党团组织作出了贡献。

The CPC and the Communist Youth League members at SHU worked in national and municipal organizations.

上海大学学生在全国、上海党团组织中任职情况（部分）
SHU Students' Positions in National and Municipal Party and League Organizations (Partial)

姓　名	职　务
李硕勋	全国学联总会党团书记
郭伯和	中共上海小沙渡部委书记
糜文浩	中共上海区委沪西部委组织委员
康　生	中共上海沪中、闸北、沪西、沪东区委书记
顾作霖	中共杨树浦部委委员、共青团杨树浦部委书记
贺　昌	共青团上海地委书记
阳翰笙	中共上海闸北区委书记、共青团上大支部书记
曾延生	中共引翔港部委宣传委员、共青团上海地委引翔港部委书记
贺威圣	共青团闸北部委书记

李硕勋（1903—1931），四川庆符（今高县）人。1923年底进入上海大学学习。先后任第七届全国学生联合会总会会长兼党团书记、第八届全国学联总会会长。1931年在中共广东省军委书记任内被国民党当局逮捕，英勇就义。

Li Shuoxun (1903-1931) entered SHU in 1923. He chaired the All-China Students' Federation.

顾作霖（1908—1934），江苏嘉定（今属上海）人。1925年7月进入上海大学学习。1926年初任中共杨树浦部委委员、共青团杨树浦部委书记。在1934年1月召开的中共六届五中全会上当选为中共中央委员、中央政治局委员，后任红军总政治部代理主任兼第一方面军野战政治部主任。同年5月28日病逝于瑞金。

Gu Zuolin (1908-1934) entered SHU in 1925. He was Secretary of Yangshupu Communist Youth League in 1926.

1931年11月，苏区中央局委员摄于第一次全苏大会。左起：顾作霖、任弼时、朱德、邓发、项英、毛泽东、王稼祥
From left to right: Gu Zuolin, Ren Bishi, Zhu De, Deng Fa, Xiang Ying, Mao Zedong, and Wang Jiaxiang

贺昌（1906—1935），山西离石柳林（今属山西柳林）人。1923年9月进入上海大学学习。1925年任中国共产主义青年团中央执委会委员、中央局成员，10月兼任共青团上海地委书记。1934年中央主力红军长征后奉命在赣南坚持游击战争，任中共中央苏区分局委员、中央军区政治部主任。1935年3月牺牲于江西会昌。

He Chang (1906-1935) entered SHU in 1923. He was a member of the Executive Committee of Shanghai Communist Youth League in 1925.

（十二）创办进步和革命报刊
Founding Progressive and Revolutionary Newspapers

上海大学在办学过程中，创办了一系列的报刊。这些报刊既包括上海大学的校报，也有学生会主办的报纸，还包括各类学生社团主办的杂志。除了个别的纯文学刊物外，其中大多数报刊紧密联系校园生活和社会革命运动实际，阐发师生的进步思想和革命主张，传播马克思列宁主义理论，拥护孙中山"联俄、联共、扶助农工"的三大政策，推动国民革命运动发展，批判政治上的反动思潮。这些报刊的出版，扩大了上海大学在社会上的影响，也使一大批学生在这些刊物的编发过程中受到了锻炼。

SHU started a series of newspapers and periodicals, which promoted the social influence of SHU and cultivated talents in media management.

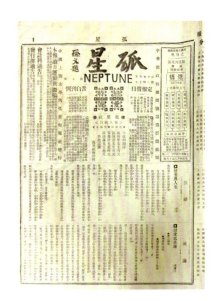

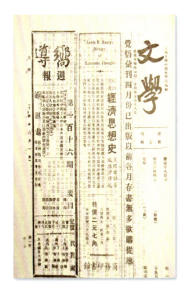

《孤星》为上海大学中国孤星社主办的旬刊。

Neptune was sponsored by the Neptune Association of SHU.

《文学》为上海大学中国文学系编辑，作为《民国日报》的文艺副刊之一随报发行。自 1925 年 4 月 27 日创刊至 6 月 9 日停刊，共出版了 6 期。

Literature, started on April 27, 1925, edited by the Chinese Literature Department of SHU.

《上海大学周刊》为上海大学校刊。陈望道为编辑主任。于右任的《〈上海大学一览〉弁言》和邓中夏的《上大的使命》就发表在第一期上。

Shanghai University Weekly was the school newspaper, Chen Wangdao serving as the head editor.

《台州评论》为上海大学台州同乡会主办的刊物。在 1926 年 6 月 1 日出版的第四期上，发表了张崇德的《为最近北方政变告台州民众》一文。

Taizhou Review was sponsored by Taizhou Association of SHU.

《上大五卅特刊》为上海大学学生会在五卅运动爆发后创办的特刊。1925 年 6 月 15 日创刊，共出 8 期。刊头由校长于右任题写。

The Special Issue of Shanghai University for the May Thirtieth Movement started on June 15, 1925, run by SHU Students Union.

《中山主义》为上海大学中山主义研究会主办的周刊。1925 年 12 月 20 日创刊，是上海大学宣传革命的三民主义的一个阵地。由瞿秋白演讲，秦邦宪、崔小立记录的《国民革命与阶级争斗》就发表在第一期上。

Sun Yat-sen's Doctrine, sponsored by Sun Yat-sen's Doctrine Research Institute of SHU, was published on December 20, 1925.

《上大附中》为上海大学附中学生会主办的半月刊。1925 年五卅运动之前出版了 3 期，后因五卅运动中学校被封而一度停刊，1925 年 10 月复刊。

Affiliated High School of Shanghai University was sponsored by the affiliated school's Students Union.

《圣诞节的敬礼》为上海大学附中非基督教同盟编辑的宣传反对基督教言论的小册子。1925 年 12 月 25 日出版，其中刊登有《上大附中非基同盟宣言》等文章。

The Christmas Salute, compiled by the Affiliated High School of SHU, was published on December 25, 1925.

教学名师与演讲名人

Outstanding Professors and Renowned Orators

上海大学从创办伊始，就注重延聘名师和名人来校任教和演讲，这对上海大学学务的改进、教育质量和声望的提升、影响的扩大及学生的培养起到了十分重要的作用。

Since its inception, SHU had attached great importance to recruiting outstanding scholars, which had played a significant role in improving the education quality and enhancing the social influence of SHU.

（一）教学名师
Outstanding Professors

丰子恺（1898—1975），浙江桐乡人。1923年到上海大学任教。新中国成立后，任上海中国画院院长、中国美术家协会上海分会主席等职。

Feng Zikai (1898-1975) became a professor of SHU in 1923. After the founding of the PRC, he was appointed Dean of Shanghai Chinese Painting Academy and Chairman of the Shanghai Branch of the Chinese Artists Association.

田汉（1898—1968），湖南长沙人。1923年秋到上海大学任教。新中国成立后，任文化部戏曲改进局、艺术局局长等职。

Tian Han (1898-1968) became a professor of SHU in 1923. After the founding of the PRC, he was appointed Director of Drama Improvement Bureau, Director of Art Bureau of the Ministry of Culture, etc.

任弼时（1904—1950），湖南湘阴（今汨罗）人。马克思列宁主义者，无产阶级革命家、政治家、组织家，中国共产党、中国人民解放军的主要领导人。1924年夏到上海大学任教。历中共第七届中央政治局委员、中央书记处书记等职。1950年10月27日在北京逝世。

Ren Bishi (1904-1950) became a professor of SHU in 1924. He served successively as a member of the Seventh Political Bureau of the CPC Central Committee and a member of the CPC Central Commitee Secretariat.

※ 前面已作过介绍的教师不再列入，此处介绍以姓氏笔画为序
Outsanding professors, by stroke order in the surname, with the aforementioned names excluded

刘大白（1880—1932），浙江绍兴人。中国现代著名诗人、文学史家。1924年春到上海大学任教。1932年病逝。

Liu Dabai (1880-1932) was a famous poet and literary historian. He became a professor of SHU in 1924.

朱自清（1898—1948），祖籍浙江绍兴，生于江苏东海（今属连云港）。中国现代散文家、诗人、学者、民主战士。1924年前后到上海大学任教。1948年8月病逝。

Zhu Ziqing (1898-1948), a professor of SHU around 1924, was a well-known modern essayist, poet, and scholar as well as a fighter for democracy.

何世桢（1896—1975），安徽望江人。获美国密歇根大学法学博士学位。1924年春到上海大学任教。持志大学创办人之一。1975年病逝于扬州。

He Shimei (1896-1975) became a professor of SHU in 1924. He received his Juris Doctor's Degree from the University of Michigan, and was one of the founders of Chizhi University.

李汉俊（1890—1927），湖北潜江人。中国共产党第一次全国代表大会代表。1925年春到上海大学任教。1927年12月被桂系军阀胡宗铎杀害。

Li Hanjun (1890-1927) became a professor of SHU in 1925. He was one of the delegates of the First National Congress of the CPC.

杨杏佛（1893—1933），江西清江（今属樟树）人。1923年前后到上海大学任教。1933年6月18日，被国民党当局暗杀。

Yang Xingfo (1893-1933) became a professor of SHU around 1923.

沈观澜（1902—1965），又名沈志远，浙江萧山人。1926年前后到上海大学任教。新中国成立后，当选为中国科学院哲学科学部学部委员，任上海市政协副主席等职。

Shen Guanlan (1902-1965) became a professor of SHU around 1926. After the founding of the PRC, he was elected Member of the Faculty of Philosophy and Science, the Chinese Academy of Sciences.

周水平（1894—1926），江苏江阴人。1924年前后到上海大学任教。1926年1月被军阀孙传芳下令杀害。同年11月25日，毛泽东以"润之"的笔名发表《江浙农民的痛苦及其反抗运动》一文，对周水平作出高度评价。

Zhou Shuiping (1894-1926) became a professor of SHU around 1924. Mao Zedong published an artilce to highly recognize Zhou on his sacrifice on November 25, 1926.

周建人（1888—1984），浙江绍兴人。1924年春到上海大学任教。新中国成立后，任全国人大常委会副委员长，全国政协副主席，中国共产党第九至第十一届中央委员，第六、第七届民进中央主席。

Zhou Jianren (1888-1984) became a professor of SHU in 1924. After the founding of the PRC, he served as Vice Chairman of the Standing Committee of the National People's Congress and Vice Chairman of the CPPCC.

第一部分　1922—1927 年的上海大学　　　　　　　　　三、教学名师与演讲名人

郑振铎（1898—1958），祖籍福建长乐，生于浙江温州。1926年前后到上海大学任教。新中国成立后，任文化部副部长、文物局局长等职。

Zheng Zhenduo (1898-1958) became a professor of SHU in 1926. After the founding of the PRC, he served as Director of the Cultural Relics Bureau of the Ministry of Culture, Vice Minister of Culture, etc.

俞平伯（1900—1990），浙江德清人。1923年秋到上海大学任教。新中国成立后，任北京大学教授、中国社会科学院文学研究所研究员等职。

Yu Pingbo (1900-1990) became a professor of SHU in 1923. After the founding of the PRC, he served as a professor of Peking University, a researcher of the Institute of Literature of the Chinese Academy of Social Sciences, etc.

胡朴安（1878—1947），安徽泾县人。1924年春到上海大学任教。抗战胜利后，任上海通志馆馆长、上海文献委员会主任等职。

Hu Puan (1878-1947) became a professor of SHU in 1924.

萧朴生（1897—1926），四川德阳人。邓小平的入团介绍人之一。1925年8月到上海大学任教。1926年4月任中华全国济难会党团书记。1926年病逝。

Xiao Pusheng (1897-1926) became a professor of SHU in 1925. He introduced Deng Xiaoping to join the League.

赵景深（1902—1985），祖籍四川宜宾，生于浙江丽水。1925年9月到上海大学任教。新中国成立后，任复旦大学教授、中国古代戏曲研究会会长、中国民间文学研究会上海分会主席等职。

Zhao Jingshen (1902-1985) became a professor of SHU in 1925.

校长于右任聘请赵景深为中国文学系教授的聘书

Appointment Letter of Zhao Jingshen as a professor of the Chinese Literature Department of SHU

傅东华（1893—1971），浙江金华人。1924年春到上海大学任教。新中国成立后，任中国文字改革委员会研究员、中华书局编审、《辞海》语辞学科主编等职。

Fu Donghua (1893-1971), a professor of SHU from 1924, was Chief Editor for *Ci Hai*, a comprehensive Chinese dictionary, etc.

彭述之（1895—1983），湖南邵阳人。1924年8月到上海大学任教，一度兼任社会学系主任。1973年移居美国。1983年病逝。

Peng Shuzhi (1895-1983) became a professor of SHU in 1924. He once served as Dean of the Sociology Department of SHU.

蒋光慈（1901—1931），祖籍安徽六安（一说河南固始），生于安徽霍邱。1924年8月到上海大学任教。1926年中篇小说《少年飘泊者》问世，在读者中引起很大反响，习仲勋、陶铸、胡耀邦等无产阶级革命家都深受这部作品的影响。1931年8月病逝。

Jiang Guangci (1901-1931) was a writer and became a professor of SHU in 1924. He published the novella *Youth Vagrant* in 1926.

蒋光慈《少年飘泊者》书影
Youth Vagrant by Jiang Guangci

谢六逸（1898—1945），贵州贵阳人。1926年前后到上海大学任教。为中国现代新闻教育事业的奠基者之一。1945年病逝。

Xie Liuyi (1898-1945), a professor of SHU around 1926, was one of the founders of modern journalism education of China.

曹聚仁（1900—1972），浙江浦江人。记者、作家。1925年3月到上海大学任教。抗日战争时期任战地记者，曾报道淞沪战役、台儿庄战役。1950年任新加坡《南洋商报》驻香港特派记者。后多次回内地，促进祖国统一事业。1972年病逝于澳门。

Cao Juren (1900-1972) began to teach at SHU in 1925. He was a journalist and writer, and field reporter during the Anti-Japanese War.

（二）演讲名人
Renowned Orators

马君武（1881—1940），祖籍湖北蒲圻，生于广西桂林。中国近代获得德国工学博士第一人。曾任孙中山革命政府秘书长、广西省省长，担任过北洋政府司法总长、教育总长。1923年5月13日在上海大学作"国民生计政策"演讲。

Ma Junwu (1881-1940) gave a lecture on "National Livelihood Policy" at SHU on May 13, 1923. He was the first Chinese who obtained a doctor's degree in engineering in Germany. He once served as Secretary-General of Sun Yat-sen's Revolutionary Government and Minister of Education of the Government of the Chinese Republic.

刘仁静（1902—1987），湖北应城人。1921年出席中国共产党第一次全国代表大会。1924年4月17日在上海大学作演讲。新中国成立后，在北京师范大学任教。后任人民出版社特约翻译、国务院参事。

Liu Renjing (1902-1987) gave a lecture at SHU on April 17, 1924. He attended the First National Congress of the Communist Party of China in 1921.

吴玉章（1878—1966），四川荣县人。无产阶级革命家、教育家。1925年11月19日在上海大学作"民族问题与阶级争斗"演讲。

Wu Yuzhang (1878-1966), an educator and proletarian revolutionist, gave a lecture on "National Issues and Class Struggle" at SHU on November 19, 1925.

吴稚晖（1865—1953），江苏武进（今属常州）人。国民党元老。1927年4月在上海大学作"注音字母"讲座。1953年在台湾逝世。

Wu Zhihui (1865-1953), a veteran KMT member, gave a lecture on "Sound-Notating Alphabet" at SHU in April 1927.

沈玄庐（1883—1928），浙江萧山人。1924年7月在上海大学作"外交问题"讲座。1928年8月被暗杀。

Shen Xuanlu (1883-1928) gave a lecture on "Diplomatic Issues" at SHU in July 1924.

胡适（1891—1962），祖籍安徽绩溪，生于江苏川沙（今属上海浦东新区）。1923年11月11日在上海大学作"科学与人生观"演讲。1962年2月在台北病逝。

Hu Shi (1891-1962) gave a lecture on "Science and Outlook on Life" at SHU on November 11, 1923. He served as Chinese Ambassador to the United States (1938-1942).

胡愈之（1896—1986），浙江上虞人。1924年7月在上海大学作"世界语"讲座。新中国成立后，任国家出版总署署长、全国人大常委会副委员长等职。

Hu Yuzhi (1896-1986) gave a lecture on "Esperanto" at SHU in July 1924. After the founding of the PRC, he served as Director of the National Publishing Administration, Vice Chairman of the Standing Committee of the National People's Congress, etc.

郭沫若（1892—1978），四川乐山人。1925年5月2日在上海大学作"文艺之社会的使命"演讲。新中国成立后，任政务院副总理、中国科学院院长兼哲学社会科学部主任、全国人大常委会副委员长、全国政协副主席等职。

Guo Moruo (1892-1978) gave a lecture on "Social Mission of Literature and Art" at SHU on May 2, 1925. After the founding of the PRC, he served as Director of the Department of Philosophy and Social Sciences and President of the Chinese Academy of Sciences, Vice Chairman of the National Committee of the CPPCC, etc.

章太炎（1869—1936），浙江余杭人。1923年12月2日在上海大学作"中国语音系统"讲座。1935年在苏州主持章氏国学讲习会。1936年6月病逝。

Zhang Taiyan (1869-1936), a master of Chinese culture, gave a lecture on "Chinese Phonetic Symbol System" at SHU on December 2, 1923.

戴季陶（1891—1949），祖籍浙江吴兴（今属湖州），生于四川广汉。国民党元老。1924年7月在上海大学作"东方问题与世界问题"演讲。曾任黄埔军校政治部主任、中山大学校长、国民党中宣部部长、考试院院长等职。1949年自杀身亡。

Dai Jitao (1891-1949), a veteran KMT member, gave a lecture on "Oriental Issues and World Issues" at SHU in July 1924. He served as President of Sun Yat-Sen University, etc.

知名学生
Notable Alumni

上海大学践行"养成建国人才，促进文化事业"的办学宗旨，取得了令人瞩目的成就。他们中有中国共产党的领导人，有为国捐躯的烈士，有著名的社会活动家，有一流的学者、作家、剧作家、诗人等，在马克思主义理论传播、社会科学研究、自然科学普及等方面都作出了杰出的贡献。也有个别人在后来的人生道路中背离了求学时的初心。

SHU made remarkable achievements in the talent cultivation by diligently practicing its tenet—Cultivating National Leaders and Promoting Cultural Undertakings. There was a wealth of young talents at SHU. Some were outstanding leaders of the CPC, martyrs, distinguished social activists, or first-rate scholars or writers. They made prominent contributions to the spread of Marxism, social sciences research, and the popularization of natural sciences in China. And a few of them betrayed the original aspirations in their later life.

丁玲（1904—1986），原名丁冰之，湖南常德人。作家、社会活动家。1923年8月进入上海大学学习。其创作的长篇小说《太阳照在桑干河上》于1952年获苏联斯大林文艺奖金。

Ding Ling (1904-1986) was a writer and social activist. She entered SHU in 1923. Her novel *The Sun Shines over the Sanggan River* was awarded the Stalin Prize for Literature in 1952.

王步文（1898—1931），安徽岳西人。1924年进入上海大学学习。1930年任安徽省委书记，是中共安徽省委第一任书记。1931年英勇就义。

Wang Buwen (1898-1931) entered SHU in 1924. He was the first Secretary of the CPC Anhui Provincial Committee in 1930.

王稼祥（1906—1974），安徽泾县人。无产阶级革命家。1925年8月进入上海大学学习。1931年任红军总政治部主任、中央革命军事委员会副主席等职。新中国成立后，任首任驻苏联大使、外交部副部长、中共中央对外联络部部长等职。

Wang Jiaxiang (1906-1974) entered SHU in 1925. After the founding of the PRC, he served as the first Ambassador to the Soviet Union, Deputy Minister of Foreign Affairs, etc.

孔另境（1904—1972），原名令俊，浙江桐乡人。作家、出版家。1923年进入上海大学学习。新中国成立后，任山东齐鲁大学教授、春明书店总编辑、上海出版文献资料编辑所编审等职。

Kong Lingjing (1904-1972), a writer and publisher, entered SHU in 1923.

※ 前面已作过介绍的学生不再列入，此处介绍以姓氏笔画为序

Notable Alumni, by stroke order in the surname, with the aforementioned names excluded

第一部分　1922—1927 年的上海大学

四、知名学生

龙大道（1901—1931），原名龙康庄，字坦之，贵州锦屏人。1923 年进入上海大学学习。1931 年 2 月 2 日遇害，是"龙华二十四烈士"之一。

Long Dadao (1901-1931) was one of the "24 Longhua Martyrs." He entered SHU in 1923.

匡亚明（1906—1996），江苏丹阳人。1926 年进入上海大学学习。新中国成立后，任吉林大学党委书记兼校长、南京大学党委书记兼校长、国家古籍整理出版规划小组组长等职。

Kuang Yaming (1906-1996) entered SHU in 1926. After the founding of the PRC, he served as President and Secretary of the Party Committee of Jilin University, President and Secretary of the Party Committee of Nanjing University, etc.

刘披云（1905—1983），又名刘荣简，四川广安人。1925 年进入上海大学学习。新中国成立后，任南开大学党委书记兼副校长、云南省副省长、云南大学党委书记兼校长等职。

Liu Piyun (1905-1983) entered SHU in 1925. After the founding of the PRC, he served as Vice President of Nankai University, President of Yunnan University, etc.

关向应（1902—1946），原名致祥，辽宁金县（今大连金州）人。1924 年 5 月进入上海大学学习。1934 年 10 月与贺龙、任弼时创建了湘鄂川黔革命根据地。抗日战争全面爆发后，任八路军 120 师政委。1946 年 7 月在延安病逝。

Guan Xiangying (1902-1946) was a proletarian revolutionist. He entered SHU in 1924. He commanded the Red Army and established Hunan-Hubei-Sichuan-Guizhou Revolutionary Base with He Long and Ren Bishi.

严信民（1902—1988），陕西澄城人。1923年前后进入上海大学学习。1949年任北平市人民政府研究室主任。新中国成立后，任中央民族学院副院长、中国农工民主党中央副主席等职。

Yan Xinmin (1902-1988) entered SHU around 1923.

杨尚昆（1907—1998），四川潼南（今属重庆）人。1926年5月进入上海大学学习。1934年任红三军团政委。新中国成立后，任中共中央办公厅主任、中共中央军委常务副主席兼秘书长、中央政治局委员等职。1988年4月当选为中华人民共和国主席。

Yang Shangkun (1907-1998) entered SHU in 1926. In 1988, he was elected President of the PRC.

李士群（1907—1943），浙江遂昌人。1924年前后进入上海大学学习。曾参加中国共产党。1932年被捕叛变。1938年沦为汉奸。1943年9月被日本人毒死。

Li Shiqun (1907-1943) entered SHU around 1924. He betrayed the CPC in 1932 and became a traitor in 1938. He was prisoned to death by the Japanese in 1943.

李伯钊（1911—1985），四川重庆（今重庆市）人。戏剧家。1926年进入上海大学学习。新中国成立后，任北京人民艺术剧院院长、中央戏剧学院副院长。著有歌剧《长征》、话剧《北上》等。

Li Bozhao (1911-1985) entered SHU in 1926. After the founding of the PRC, she served as President of Beijing People's Art Theater and Vice President of the Central Academy of Drama.

何挺颖（1905—1929），陕西南郑（今属汉中）人。1925年6月进入上海大学学习。1927年9月参加秋收起义和三湾改编，任工农革命军第一团党代表，参加了黄洋界保卫战等战斗。1929年1月在江西大庾战斗中负伤牺牲。

He Tingying(1905-1929) entered SHU in 1925.

余泽鸿（1903—1935），四川长宁人。1924年6月进入上海大学学习。1929年夏任中共中央秘书长。1935年12月在长征途中为了掩护主力红军，牺牲于四川江安。

Yu Zehong (1903-1935) entered SHU in 1924. He was appointed Secretary-General of the CPC Central Committee in 1929.

张仲实（1903—1987），陕西陇县人。马列主义著作翻译家、马克思主义理论家。1926年进入上海大学学习。新中国成立后，曾任中共中央马恩列斯著作编译局副局长。

Zhang Zhongshi (1903-1987) was a Marxist theorist and translator of Marxist-Leninist works. He entered SHU in 1926.

张崇文（1906—1995），浙江临海人。中华人民共和国开国少将。1926年1月进入上海大学学习。新中国成立后，任中国人民解放军国防科学委员会副秘书长、铁道兵政治部副主任、顾问，全国政协委员。

Zhang Chongwen (1906-1995) was a Founding General of the PRC. He entered SHU in 1926.

陈明（1902—1941），福建龙岩人。1926年秋进入上海大学学习。1934年10月参加长征。抗日战争中任八路军115师政治部宣传部部长。1941年11月在与日军作战中牺牲。

Chen Ming (1902-1941) entered SHU in 1926.

陈伯达（1904—1989），字尚友，福建惠安人。1924年9月进入上海大学学习。1966年任"中央文化革命小组"组长，为中共九届中央政治局常委。1973年被开除党籍，撤销党内外一切职务。1981年被判刑。1989年去世。

Chen Boda (1904-1989) entered SHU in 1924. In 1973, he was expelled from the CPC and dismissed from all his posts both inside and outside the Party.

周文在（1906—1994），江苏常熟人。中华人民共和国开国少将。1925年进入上海大学学习。新中国成立后，任福建省军区副政治委员、江苏省政协副主席等职。

Zhou Wenzai (1906-1994) was a Founding General of the PRC. He entered SHU in 1925.

孟超（1902—1976），山东诸城人。诗人、剧作家。1924年进入上海大学学习。新中国成立后，任国家出版总署图书馆副馆长、戏剧出版社副总编辑、人民文学出版社副总编辑等职。曾创作历史剧《李慧娘》。

Meng Chao (1902-1976) was a poet and dramatist. He entered SHU in 1924.

武止戈（1902—1933），陕西渭南人。1924 年初进入上海大学学习。1932 年任中共张家口特委委员，推动和协助冯玉祥建立抗日同盟军。1933 年 10 月在对日战斗中被炸弹击中殉国。

Wu Zhige (1902-1933) entered SHU in 1924.

罗尔纲（1901—1997），广西贵县人。历史学家。1926 年进入上海大学学习。新中国成立后，任中国社会科学院近代史研究所一级研究员。

Luo Ergang (1901-1997) entered SHU in 1926.

施蛰存（1905—2003），浙江杭州人。著名学者。1923 年进入上海大学学习，同年 10 月 23 日在《民国日报》副刊《觉悟》上发表《上海大学的精神》。新中国成立后，任华东师范大学教授。

Shi Zhecun (1905-2003) entered SHU in 1923.

胡允恭（1902—1991），又名胡萍舟，安徽寿县人。1923 年进入上海大学学习。新中国成立后，任福建师范学院院长、南京大学教授。

Hu Yungong (1902-1991) entered SHU in 1923. After the founding of the PRC, he was President of Fujian Normal University and a professor at Nanjing University.

秦邦宪（1907—1946），又名博古，江苏无锡人。1925 年 9 月进入上海大学学习。1931 年 9 月起为中共临时中央局成员、临时中央局政治局书记和负责人。同王明一起犯了"左"倾错误。1937 年后任新华社社长、中共中央组织部部长。1941 年后在延安创办并主持《解放日报》和新华社工作。1946 年 4 月 8 日因飞机失事遇难。

Qin Bangxian (1907-1946) was a leader of the CPC. He entered SHU in 1925. He was appointed President of Xinhua News Agency and Minister of the Organization Department of the CPC Central Committee after 1937.

郭毅（1905—1942），又名郭君毅，江苏南汇（今属上海浦东新区）人。1924年进入上海大学学习。1926年9、10月间根据党组织安排，到武昌考入北伐军前敌总指挥部政治训练班并加入北伐军。1942年9月被国民党忠义救国军杀害。

Guo Yi (1905-1942) entered SHU in 1924.

蔡威（1907—1936），福建宁德人。1925年进入上海大学学习。1931年10月初由党中央派到鄂豫皖苏区筹建电台通讯工作。1933年初任红四方面军总指挥部第二台台长。1935年7月任中国工农红军总司令部第二局局长。1936年9月病逝于长征途中。

Cai Wei (1907-1936) entered SHU in 1925.

谭其骧（1911—1992），浙江嘉善人。中国历史地理学的主要奠基人之一。1926年进入上海大学学习。新中国成立后，任复旦大学教授，当选中国科学院学部委员。

Tan Qixiang (1911-1992) was one of the main founders of Chinese historical geography. He entered SHU in 1926 and was elected Member of the Chinese Academy of Sciences after the founding of the PRC.

薛尚实（1902—1977），广东梅州人。1926年进入上海大学学习。1927年加入上海大学学生军，参加了上海工人第三次武装起义。新中国成立后，任青岛市委书记、同济大学党委书记兼校长等职。

Xue Shangshi (1902-1977) entered SHU in 1926. After the founding of the PRC, he served as Secretary of the CPC Qingdao Municipal Committee, President of Tongji University, etc.

戴望舒（1905—1950），浙江余杭人。诗人。1923年秋进入上海大学学习。诗歌名作《雨巷》曾传诵一时。1949年8月任新闻出版总署国际新闻局法文科主任，从事编译工作。1950年在北京病逝。

Dai Wangshu (1905-1950) was a poet, known for his poem "A Lane in the Rain." He entered SHU in 1923.

追认学籍　筹划复校

Recognition of Student Status and Re-operation of SHU

上海大学于 1927 年 5 月被国民党当局封闭以后，近两千名学生在就业、晋升等方面受到不公正待遇。上海大学老校长、时任国民党中常委和监察院院长的于右任为争取上海大学学生的大学学籍资格，与国民党当局一再交涉。1936 年 3 月在国民党中央常务委员会第八次会议上，通过"追认上海大学学生学籍，与国立大学同等待遇"的决定。

After SHU was closed by the KMT authorities in May 1927, the Ministry of Education of the KMT Government refused to recognize the student status of SHU. In view of such unfair treatments, Yu Youren, President of SHU, repeatedly negotiated with the authorities, and finally in March 1936, at the eighth meeting of the KMT Central Standing Committee, SHU won back the official recognition of student status and equal treatments with national universities.

（一）"追认上海大学学生学籍，与国立大学同等待遇"
Winning Back Recognition of Student Status and Equal Treatments

1936年，上海大学学生代表马文彦等致函于右任"请转呈中央请求追认上海大学学生学籍"，回忆创办经过："（一）上大之创办既经请命于总理，总理且亲任该校之董事长，本党先进诸公多曾担任校董、讲授，即先生之出任校长亦为总理所任命；（二）上大经费曾经中央党部决议由国民政府按月拨给；（三）上大之成立曾在国民政府立案。"

According to some students' recollection in 1936, in the early years of SHU, Sun Yat-sen acted as the board chairman and appointed Yu Youren President, and the university was subsidized with the KMT governmental fund on a monthly basis.

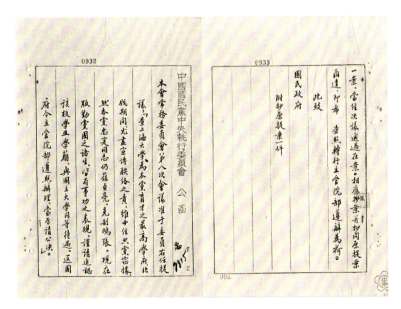

国民党中央常务委员会第八次会议通过于右任关于"追认上海大学学生学籍，与国立大学同等待遇"议案之公函

Approval Letter of President Yu Youren's proposal on "Recognition of Student Status of SHU Students and Equal Treatments with National Universities"

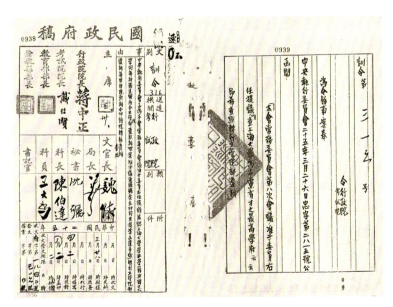

国民政府就国民党中央执行委员会关于"追认上海大学学生学籍，与国立大学同等待遇"决议，送达国民政府行政院、考试院之训令

KMT Government's Resolution on the "Recognition of Student Status of SHU Students and Equal Treatments with National Universities"

（二）成立上海大学同学会
Establishing SHU Alumni Associations

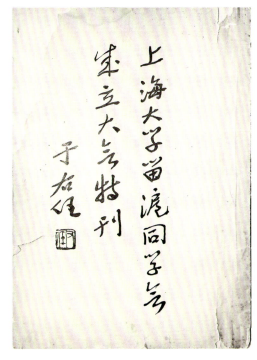

1936年9月上海大学留沪同学会成立。图为《上海大学留沪同学会成立大会特刊》封面，于右任题刊名
Cover of *The Special Issue on Establishing Shanghai University Alumni Association in Shanghai*, inscribed by Yu Youren, 1936

20世纪50年代台北市上海大学同学会成立。图为成立大会留影，于右任出席
The inauguration of the Shanghai University Alumni Association in Taipei in the 1950s, attended by Yu Youren

（三）持续不断地进行上海大学的复校工作
Efforts on Re-operation of SHU

从 1936 年 3 月国民党中央常务委员会第八次会议通过"追认上海大学学生学籍，与国立大学同等待遇"的决定后，于右任一直在推动上海大学的复校工作，多次到上海召集校友讨论上海大学复校的具体事宜。

Since the eighth meeting of the KMT Central Standing Committee in March 1936, Yu Youren had been pushing the resumption of SHU and organizing the alumni in Shanghai to discuss related issues.

1945 年 9 月 17 日《申报》刊登《上海大学复校招生》的简讯
"Notice on Re-enrollment: Shanghai University," reported by *Shun Pao*, September 17, 1945

1947 年 6 月 30 日《申报》刊登《二十年前旧学府上海大学将重建》的消息
"Shanghai University to Be Re-operated," reported by *Shun Pao*, June 30, 1947

1945 年 10 月 9 日《民国日报》刊登《于右任校长电促上海大学复校》的报道
"Yu Youren Urges to Re-operate Shanghai University," reported by *The Republican Daily*, October 9, 1945

附

汪伪时期的"国立上海大学"
（1941—1945 年）

Appendix: The Puppet "National Shanghai University"
(1941-1945)

1941 年 9 月 20 日，汪伪政府盗用上海大学校名，成立伪"国立上海大学"，在"中日两国合办"的幌子下为日本侵略者在中国教育领域推行奴化教育服务。该校进步师生在中国共产党和上海学联的领导下，积极参与旨在反抗日本帝国主义法西斯统治和奴化教育政策的"助学运动"和迎接全民族抗战胜利的"天亮运动"。1945 年 8 月 15 日，日本宣布投降，伪"国立上海大学"随之停办。

On September 20, 1941, the Wang Jingwei puppet government misappropriated the name of SHU and established the puppet "National Shanghai University," which kept promoting slavery education in China for Japanese invaders. Under the leadership of the CPC and the Shanghai Students' Federation, the teachers and students of the puppet "National Shanghai University" actively participated in underground anti-Japanese activities. On August 15, 1945, Japan announced its surrender, and then the puppet "National Shanghai University" ceased operation.

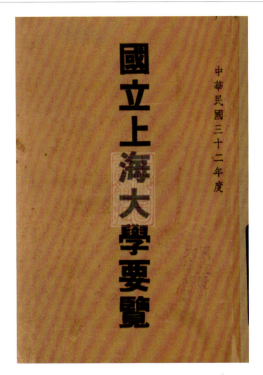

1943年出版的"国立上海大学要览"
"Survey of National Shanghai University," 1943

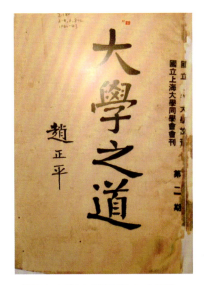

"国立上海大学同学会会刊"
"The Special Issue of National Shanghai University Alumni Association"

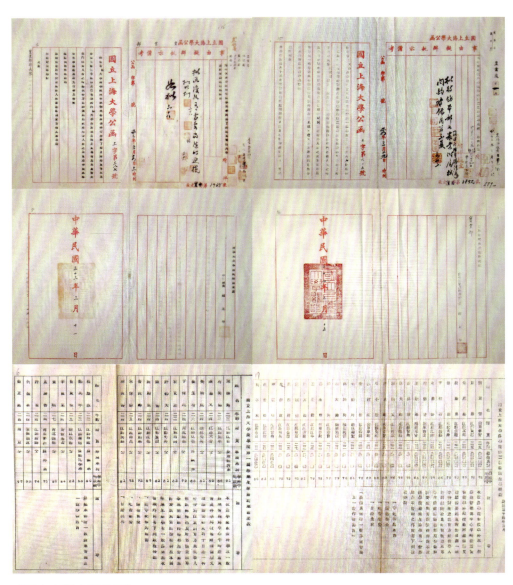

"国立上海大学公函"
"Letter of National Shanghai University"

第二部分

1958—1994 年的"四校"

　　20 世纪 50 年代中期，上海作出工业生产向高（级）、精（密）、尖（端）方向发展的决策，由此急需大批这方面的高级专门人才，1958—1960 年，上海科学技术大学、上海计算技术学校（上海科技高等专科学校前身）和上海工学院（上海工业大学前身）相继成立。20 世纪 80 年代改革开放初期，上海进入经济社会转型发展轨道，需要大批既有理工基础又有人文社会科学专业知识的复合型、应用型人才，1983 年，上海五所大学分校和上海市美术学校合并组建成上海大学。

Part II

"Four Institutions" in 1958-1994

From 1958 to 1960, Shanghai University of Science and Technology, Shanghai School of Computing Technology (the predecessor of Shanghai College of Science and Technology), and Shanghai Institute of Technology (the predecessor of Shanghai University of Technology) were founded successively. In 1983, by merging Shanghai Fine Arts College and five branches of existing institutions, Shanghai University was re-founded to join in the current of cultivating comprehensive talents from the reform and opening-up.

一

上海工业大学
Shanghai University of Technology (SUT)

（一）创建
Foundation

1. 学校成立　Founding of SUT

1960年7月，教育部党组批复中共上海市委，同意建立上海工学院；是月，中共上海市委同意李华担任院长兼党委书记；9月，举行上海工学院成立暨开学典礼。1972年4月，学院部分专业并入上海科学技术大学，其余大部分与上海机械学院合并，成为上海机械学院（总部）。1979年1月，经国务院批准，恢复上海工学院建制，改名为上海工业大学，中共上海市委任命张华为党委书记。1982年9月，中共中央组织部同意钱伟长担任上海工业大学校长。

In July 1960, the Party Leadership Group of the Ministry of Education approved the establishment of Shanghai Institute of Technology. In January 1979, Shanghai Institute of Technology was renamed SUT. In September 1982, the Organization Department of the Central Committee of the CPC appointed Qian Weichang to be President of SUT.

1960年9月30日，举行上海工学院成立大会暨开学典礼，教师代表朱家骏发言

The founding and opening ceremony of Shanghai Institute of Technology, September 30, 1960

2. 校园变迁　Relocations of Campuses

1960—1966 年，延长路 149 号上海工学院校门。图为首届女学生干部在校门前合影

The first batch of female student leaders in front of the gate of Shanghai Institute of Technology (1960-1966), at No. 149 Yanchang Road

1966—1972 年，上海工学院校门。图为学生在校门前合影

The students in front of the gate of Shanghai Institute of Technology (1966-1972)

张敬人，1963 年任上海工学院党委书记，1964 年兼任院长

Zhang Jingren, Secretary of the Party Committee of SUT from 1963 and concurrently President of SUT, 1964

1972—1978 年，上海机械学院校门

The gate of Shanghai Mechanical Engineering Institute (1972-1978)

1983年，上海工业大学校门
The new gate of SUT, 1983

1990年10月14日，举行庆祝建校30周年大会
Celebration of the 30th anniversary of the founding of SUT, October 14, 1990

西北小楼（1925年建，原中华浸会神学院校舍）

The Northwest Building (built in 1925)

党政办公楼——南大楼（1930年建，原晏摩氏女中校舍）

The administration building — the South Building (built in 1930)

女生宿舍——红星楼（1940年建，原中华浸会神学院校舍）

The female students' dormitory (built in 1940)

第一教学楼（1956年建，原上海交通大学分部校舍）

No. 1 Teaching Building (built in 1956)

男生宿舍（1957年建，原上海交通大学分部校舍）

The male students' dormitory (built in 1957)

图书馆（1958年建，原上海交通大学分部校舍）

The library (built in 1958)

"风雨操场"（原上海交通大学分部校舍）

The stormproof playground

1986年在"风雨操场"原址新建体育馆

The new gymnasium on the site of the stormproof playground, 1986

电机工程系实验教学楼（1961年建）
The teaching building of the Electrical Engineering Department (built in 1961)

机械工程系实验教学楼（1963年建）
The teaching building of the Mechanical Engineering Department (built in 1963)

专家招待所——乐乎楼（1984年建）
Lehu Building, the hotel (built in 1984)

3. 学校领导　Leaders of SUT

历任校（院）党委负责人一览
Party Committee Leaders

职　务	姓　名	任职年月
党委书记	李　华	1960.7—1963.2
	张敬人	1963.3—（1970.4去世）
核心小组组长	陈立富	1971.4—1973.5
党委书记	侯东升	1973.6—1978.2
	张　华	1979.4—1986.5
	郑令德	1986.6—1992.6
	吴程里	1992.6—1994.5

历任校（院）长一览
Presidents and Deans

职　务	姓　名	任职年月
院长	李　华	1960.7—1963.2
	张敬人	1964.10—（1970.4去世）
校长	杨慧洁	1979.4—1982.9
	钱伟长	1982.9—1994.5
常务副校长	徐匡迪	1986.7—1990.2
	郑令德	1990.2—1992.7
	方明伦	1992.7—1994.5

钱伟长
Qian Weichang

钱伟长（1913.10.9—2010.7.30），江苏无锡人。著名科学家、教育家，杰出的社会活动家，中国近代力学奠基人之一。1931—1937 年在清华大学物理系和研究院求学。1940 年赴加拿大多伦多大学留学，1942 年获博士学位。1942—1946 年在美国加州理工学院喷射推进实验室任研究工程师。1946 年回国，应聘为清华大学机械系教授，兼北京大学、燕京大学教授。1955 年当选为中国科学院学部委员（院士），1956 年当选为波兰科学院外籍院士。历任全国政协第六、第七、第八、第九届副主席，中国民主同盟第五、第六、第七届中央委员会副主席和第七、第八、第九届名誉主席。曾任清华大学教务长、副校长，上海工业大学校长，上海大学校长。

Qian Weichang (October 9, 1913-July 30, 2010) was a scientist, educator, academician of the Chinese Academy of Sciences, Vice Chairman of the 6th-9th National Committee of the CPPCC, Vice Chairman of the 5th-7th Central Committee of the China Democratic Leauge as well as Honorable Chairman of its 7th-9th Central Committee. He served as Provost and Vice President of Tsinghua University, President of SUT, and President of SHU.

徐匡迪
Xu Kuangdi

徐匡迪（1937.12.11— ），浙江崇德人。钢铁冶金专家，中国工程院院士、美国国家工程院外籍院士、俄罗斯工程科学院外籍院士、瑞典皇家工程院外籍院士。1959 年北京钢铁工业学院毕业后留校任教，1963 年调到上海工学院冶金工程系工作，1986 年任上海工业大学常务副校长、教授。1990—1991 年任上海市政府教卫办副主任兼高教局局长、党组书记；1991—1992 年任上海市计划委员会主任、党组书记，1992—1995 年任上海市副市长，1995—2001 年任中共上海市委副书记、市长，2002—2010 年任中国工程院院长、党组书记，2003 年当选第十届全国政协副主席。

Xu Kuangdi (December 11, 1937-), an expert in iron and steel metallurgy and academician of the Chinese Academy of Engineering, was appointed Executive Vice President of SUT in 1986. Later he served as Deputy Secretary of the CPC Shanghai Municipal Committee, Mayor of Shanghai, President of the Chinese Academy of Engineering, and Vice Chairman of the 10th CPPCC.

校党委书记张华（右）和副书记王力平
Secretary of the Party Committee Zhang Hua (right) and Deputy Secretary Wang Liping

1988年10月，校党委书记郑令德与校长钱伟长、常务副校长徐匡迪参加学校第一次系主任沙龙
Secretary of the Party Committee Zheng Lingde, President Qian Weichang, and Executive Vice President Xu Kuangdi at the first Department Chairs Saloon of SUT, 1988

4. 上级关心　Recognition of Leaders

1985 年 10 月，中共上海市委书记芮杏文到校与化学化工系学生座谈，肯定同学拟进行环境保护宣传的打算；翌月，化学化工系学生筹办的"未来属于保护环境的人们"展览会在上海市青年宫开幕，芮杏文亲临会场

Rui Xingwen, Secretary of the CPC Shanghai Municipal Committee, meeting the students of the Department of Chemical Engineering during his visit to SUT, 1985

1989 年 12 月，中共上海市委书记、市长朱镕基到校看望钱伟长校长

Zhu Rongji, Secretary of the CPC Shanghai Municipal Committee and Mayor of Shanghai, visiting President Qian Weichang at SUT, 1989

1990 年 8 月，中共中央总书记、中央军委主席江泽民为上海工业大学建校 30 周年题词

Inscription by Jiang Zemin, General Secretary of the CPC Central Committee, for the 30th anniversary of SUT, August 1990

1993年7月，在全国高校党建工作会议上被中共中央组织部、宣传部和国家教委授予"党的建设和思想政治工作先进普通高等学校"，获此殊荣的学校全国共有33所，上海仅上海工业大学1所。图为中共中央总书记、国家主席、中央军委主席江泽民与出席1993年全国高校党建工作会议代表合影。第二排右18为校党委书记吴程里

President Jiang Zemin with the representatives attending the national conference of Party building, Secretary of the Party Committee of SUT Wu Chengli in the second row. In July 1993, SUT was awarded the Prize of Party Building and Political Work by the Organization Department of the CPC Central Committee, the Publicity Department of the CPC Central Committee, and the National Education Commission. SUT was the only one that won this title in Shanghai.

1994年1月，国务院副总理李岚清来校视察，称赞学校的改革"思路对，步子大，走得稳，效果好"

In January 1994, Vice Premier Li Lanqing inspecting SUT and praising the reform of the university for its "right direction, large steps, steady development, and good results"

（二）发展
Development

1. 深化改革 Deepening Reform

1983年9月，钱伟长校长向干部、教师提出了"怎样在党的教育方针指导下，直接为改革开放中的上海市的经济建设服务"等八个"怎样办"的思考；1985年10月，他又完整地提出了办大学要拆"四堵墙"的著名思想，即要拆除学校与社会之间的墙、教学与科研之间的墙、不同学科专业之间的墙、教与学之间的墙。钱伟长校长为上海工业大学的教育教学改革指明了方向。1991年8月，上海市政府教卫办确定把上海工业大学列为上海高校综合改革试点单位。1992年6月，上海市高校改革领导小组同意上海工业大学综合改革方案及其实施步骤。

President Qian Weichang guided the educational reform of SUT. In October 1985, he put forward his thought on higher education and made clear the reform direction of SUT. In June 1992, the comprehensive reform plan was approved.

1983年9月29日，钱伟长校长在教师大会上作关于办学方向的报告
President Qian Weichang reporting on how to run SUT, September 29, 1983

1988年起，在上海高校中率先推行校系两级"任务—工资总额承包"制度和全员"目标责任制"（两年一期）。图为常务副校长徐匡迪（右）和人文社会科学部主任分别代表学校和部门签订合同

Executive Vice President Xu Kuangdi (right) signing contract with the Chair of Humanities and Social Sciences Division. In 1988, SUT took the lead among local universities in Shanghai in implementing the "Performance-Salary Contract" system and the "Target-Responsibility" system (every two years).

1992年，在上海地方高校中率先推行全员聘用合同制。图为全体新上岗的中层干部与市、校领导合影

Group photo of newly appointed cadres with Shanghai municipal and university leaders. In 1992, SUT took the lead among local universities in Shanghai in implementing the inclusive contract system.

校党委书记兼常务副校长郑令德（左）向新聘任的干部颁发岗位聘任书

Zheng Lingde (left), Secretary of the Party Committee and Executive Vice President of SUT, presenting letters of appointment to newly appointed cadres

1992年3月，创办上海工业大学科技园区，成为继东北大学以后国内第二个大学科技园区。1993年9月，经国家科委批准，上海工业大学科技园区正式列入国家级新技术开发区。

In March 1992, SUT Science and Technology Park was founded, becoming the second university science and technology park in China after Northeast University. In September 1993, with the approval of the State Science and Technology Commission, SUT Science and Technology Park was officially listed as a national new technology development zone.

科技园区
The Science and Technology Park of SUT

1993年5月，深化招生制度改革，在全国普通高校中最早推行"面向社会，自主招生，择优录取"
SUT deepened the reform of its enrollment system and became the first university in China to implement the policy of "merit-based enrollment with autonomy" in 1993.

1993年9月，深化教育教学改革，全面推行"三制"（学分制、选课制、短学期制）。图为学生在校园网上自主选课
Students choosing courses on line. In 1993, SUT deepened its educational reform and comprehensively implemented the "three systems" (namely, credit system, elective system, and short semester system).

2. 人才培养　Talent Cultivation

1984年4月，召开首届研究生思想政治工作会议，中共上海市教卫工作党委书记陈铁迪出席（右）

The first Postgraduates Development Conference of SUT, 1984

1990年，专题研讨大学生思想政治工作新体系（左三为校党委副书记赵耀华）

Deputy Secretary Zhao Yaohua (third from left) at the seminar on the new system of student cultivation at SUT, 1990

1984年1月，学校获批第一个博士学位授权点——固体力学专业；黄黔于1985年获得该专业博士学位，是上海工业大学授予博士学位的第一人（摄于1993年）

Huang Qian, the first student receiving a doctorate from SUT in 1985 (photo taken in 1993). In January 1984, solid mechanics became the first doctoral program at SUT.

钱伟长院士在指导固体力学博士点1984年招收的第一个博士生周哲玮

Academician Qian Weichang instructing Zhou Zhewei, his first doctoral student recruited at SUT

固体力学专业博士生导师刘人怀教授在上海市应用数学和力学研究所指导研究生

Professor Liu Renhuai instructing graduate students in Shanghai Institute of Applied Mathematics and Mechanics

电力传动及其自动化专业博士生导师陈伯时教授在指导青年教师
Professor Chen Boshi instructing young teachers

机械学专业博士生导师张直明教授在为研究生上课
Professor Zhang Zhiming lecturing to graduate students

钢铁冶金专业博士生导师徐匡迪教授在实验室指导研究工作

Professor Xu Kuangdi instructing research work in the laboratory

流体力学专业博士生导师戴世强教授在实验室指导研究生

Professor Dai Shiqiang instructing a graduate student in the laboratory

1985年，基础部全体员工庆祝首届教师节合影留念（背景是"北大楼"）

Group photo of staff from the Basic Education Division celebrating the first Teachers' Day, 1985

20世纪60年代，上海工学院学生按照教学计划，定期在学校机械厂参加金工实习
Students practicing in the machinery factory as per the teaching plan in the 1960s

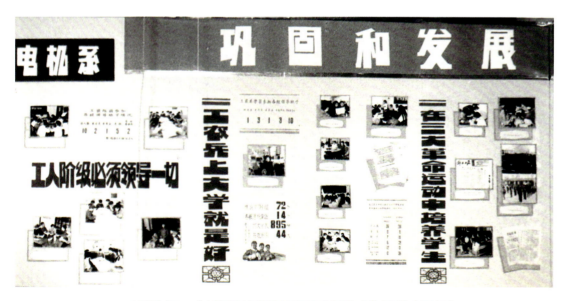

1975年，"上海机械学院教育革命展览会"展板（局部）
A display board exhibiting "Educational Revolution of Shanghai Mechanical Institute," 1975

1983年1月,钱伟长校长在电机工程系检查实验教学
President Qian Weichang visiting the Electrical Engineering Department, January 1983

1984年秋,钱伟长校长在校党委副书记王力平(左一)陪同下,检查机械工程系实验室工作
President Qian Weichang visiting the Mechanical Engineering Department, 1984

上海工业大学学生男、女篮球队是上海高校中的劲旅，1983年在上海市高校篮球联赛中双双夺魁

The men's and women's basketball teams of SUT both winning Shanghai College Basketball League, 1983

1985年10月，上海工业大学建校25周年，上海一批文化、艺术名家来校祝贺并为师生演讲（站立者前排左三：音乐家贺绿汀，右一：雕塑家张充仁，右二：书法家钱君匋，右三：美术家万籁鸣）

Famous scholars and artists visiting SUT to celebrate the 25th anniversary, 1985

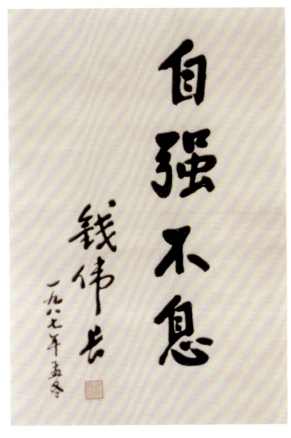

1987年，钱伟长校长手书"自强不息"，是年，学校决定以"自强不息"作为校训
President Qian Weichang's calligraphy of the SUT motto "Pursuing Excellence," 1987

1988年5月，上海市研究生科技学术协会成立大会在上海工业大学举行，钱伟长校长出席
The founding conference of Shanghai Science and Technology Academic Association for Postgraduates at SUT, 1988 (President Qian Weichang in the middle of the first row)

第二部分　1958—1994年的"四校"　　　　　　　　　　　　　　　　　　　　　　　　一、上海工业大学

1988年5月，召开上海工业大学与上海科学技术大学共建计算机学院成立大会（左起：上海科学技术大学校长郭本瑜、上海市副市长谢丽娟、上海工业大学校长钱伟长）
The founding conference for the establishment of the joint School of Computer Science by SUT and Shanghai University of Science and Technology, 1988

钱伟长校长邀请著名计算机专家、清华大学教授李三立（中）担任计算机学院院长
Li Sanli (middle), a famous computer expert and professor of Tsinghua University, invited by President Qian Weichang to serve as Dean of the School of Computer Science

1993年，举行计算机应用专业92届工程型硕士研究生毕业典礼，上海市副市长徐匡迪到会祝贺
Vice Mayor Xu Kuangdi attending the graduation ceremony for the masters of engineering in computer application to congratulate the graduates, 1993

3. 科学研究 Scientific Research

1984年5月，钱伟长院士在上海工业大学创办上海市应用数学和力学研究所并任所长

Establishment of Shanghai Institute of Applied Mathematics and Mechanics at SUT, Academician Qian Weichang appointed Director of the institute, May 1984

钱伟长院士倡导自由开放的学术氛围，力主推行Seminar制度。图为钱伟长院士在上海市应用数学和力学研究所举行的Seminar上演讲

A seminar held by Shanghai Institute of Applied Mathematics and Mechanics, advocated by Academician Qian Weichang for free and open academic atmosphere

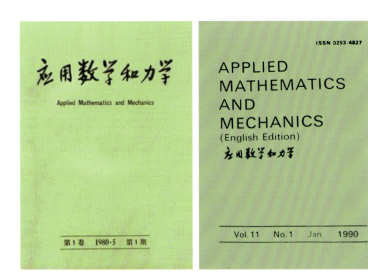

钱伟长院士于1980年创办《应用数学和力学》期刊（中、英文双刊）。图为1980年5月出版的中文刊创刊号和1990年1月出版的英文刊

Applied Mathematics and Mechanics (in both English and Chinese versions), a well-known journal founded by Academician Qian Weichang in 1980

科学研究成果获国家级奖项一览
National Achievements in Scientific Research

科研项目	奖项名称	等级	年度	获奖人
绘图曲线规	国家发明奖	四等奖	1979	杨秉烈
S76 渣油粘结剂	国家发明奖	三等奖	1985	胡彭生
直线异步电机	国家科技进步奖	二等奖	1985	江建中 蔡廷锡 艾维超 胡之光 屠关镇
低温电解渗硫技术	国家科技进步奖	三等奖	1985	余忠荪 张云倩 张万宪 李润宝 肖玉堂
叶轮机气动力学新理论体系的建立与系统研究	国家自然科学奖	二等奖	1987	刘高联
共轭曲面基础研究	国家自然科学奖	三等奖	1987	陈志新
电容式节能吊扇电机优化设计	国家科技进步奖	三等奖	1987	黄永家 杨家琪 林丁生 胡之光
石油机械难加工关键件的切削加工技术	国家科技进步奖	三等奖	1987	周家宝
地质力学地应力测量技术及应用	国家科技进步奖	三等奖	1987	潘立宙 王连捷 廖椿庭 丁原辰
流控式眼玻璃体切割器	国家发明奖	三等奖	1987	俞道义 陈银庆 俞丽和 华正清 丁仁根 姜节凯
液压油用磷氮型无灰抗磨剂制备工艺	国家发明奖	四等奖	1988	陶德华
GA-121 型整经机	国家科技进步奖	三等奖	1991	蒋洪瑶

江建中教授（左）主持的"直线异步电机"获 1985 年度国家科技进步奖二等奖

The project "Linear Asynchronous Motor," directed by Professor Jiang Jianzhong (left), winning the Second Prize of the 1985 National Prize for Progress in Science and Technology

余忠荪教授（右）主持的"低温电解渗硫技术"获 1985 年度国家科技进步奖三等奖

The project "Low Temperature Electrolysis of Sulfur Infiltration," directed by Professor Yu Zhongsun (right), winning the Third Prize of the 1985 National Prize for Progress in Science and Technology

刘高联教授的"叶轮机气动力学新理论体系的建立与系统研究"获 1987 年度国家自然科学奖二等奖

The project "The Establishment and Systematic Study of New Theoretical System of Turbomachinery Aerodynamics," directed by Professor Liu Gaolian, winning the Second Prize of the 1987 National Natural Science Award

陈志新教授的"共轭曲面基础研究"获 1987 年度国家自然科学奖三等奖

The project "Basic Research on Conjugate Surfaces," directed by Professor Chen Zhixin, winning the Third Prize of the 1987 National Natural Science Award

周家宝教授的"石油机械难加工关键件的切削加工技术"获 1987 年度国家科技进步奖三等奖

The project "Cutting Processing Technology of Key Parts in Petroleum Machinery," directed by Professor Zhou Jiabao, winning the Third Prize of the 1987 National Prize for Progress in Science and Technology

潘立宙教授（中）主持的"地质力学地应力测量技术及应用"获 1987 年度国家科技进步奖三等奖

The project "Geomechanical Geostress Measurement Technology and Application," directed by Professor Pan Lizhou (middle), winning the Third Prize of the 1987 National Prize for Progress in Science and Technology

4. 国际交流　International Exchanges

1985年，校长钱伟长和校党委书记张华会见到访的苏联科学院院士谢道夫

President Qian Weichang and Secretary of the Party Committee Zhang Hua meeting visiting Academician Leonid Ivanovich Sedov from the Soviet Academy of Sciences, 1985

1986年10月，来自海内外的王宽诚教育基金会考选委员会委员在上海工业大学合影（前排左起：钱临照、陈岱孙、汤佩松、王宽诚、陈省身、钱伟长、吴富恒，后排左起：黄贵康、费孝通、黄丽松、田长霖、张龙翔、薛寿生、王明道）

The committee members of K. C. Wong Education Foundation from home and abroad at SUT, 1986

1987年，校长钱伟长率团访问加拿大蒙特利尔大学工学院，签订两校交流与合作协议书

An agreement signed on exchange and cooperation between the Faculty of Engineering, University of Montreal, Canada and SUT, during a visit led by President Qian Weichang, 1987

1988年，法国科技代表团来校访问，副校长方明伦（前排右三）陪同参观
A French delegation of science and technology visiting SUT, accompanied by Vice President Fang Minglun (third from right in the first row), 1988

1990年，校长钱伟长为外国留学生颁发"好学生"证书
President Qian Weichang awarding the "Good Student" certificate to SUT foreign students, 1990

1990年，授予美国罗切斯特理工学院院长罗斯为上海工业大学荣誉博士
President of Rochester Institute of Technology M. Richard Rose receiving an honorary doctorate from SUT, 1990

1991年，俄罗斯教育代表团在上海市高教局局长徐匡迪（左五）的陪同下来校参观上海机器人研究所
A Russian education delegation visiting the Shanghai Robot Research Institute at SUT, 1991

获全国荣誉称号人员
Faculty Winning National Honors

荣誉称号	年度	姓名
全国教育系统劳动模范	1986	林振汉
全国教育系统劳动模范	1989	徐匡迪
全国教育系统劳动模范	1991	裴仁清
全国优秀教师	1989	张兆扬
全国优秀教师	1991	张侃谕
全国优秀教师	1993	管惠维
全国优秀教师	1993	张文俊

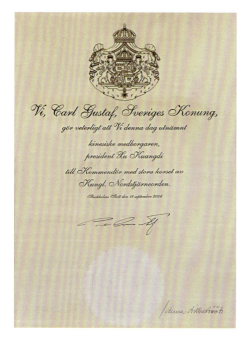

1984—1985年，徐匡迪教授赴瑞典斯堪的纳维亚·兰塞尔公司任副总工程师、技术经理。2006年，瑞典驻华大使代表瑞典国王为徐匡迪授予北极星大十字司令官勋章，以表彰他为促进瑞中友好作出的杰出贡献

In 2006, Professor Xu Kuangdi was awarded the Commander of the Grand Cross of the North Star in recognition of his outstanding contribution to promoting the friendship between Sweden and China by the Swedish Ambassador to China on behalf of the Swedish king. Professor Xu Kuangdi was invited to work as Deputy Chief Engineer and Technical Manager for an industrial corporation in Sweden from 1984 to 1985.

上海科学技术大学
Shanghai University of Science and Technology (SUST)

（一）创建
Foundation

1. 学校成立　Founding of SUST

　　1958年5月，在中共上海市委的领导下，上海市和中国科学院上海办事处共同筹办上海科学技术大学；9月，上海科学技术大学首届新生入学典礼在中国科学院上海办事处（岳阳路320号）隆重举行；翌年9月，中共上海市委任命周仁为校长、刘芳为校党委副书记兼副校长。

　　In May 1958, under the leadership of the CPC Shanghai Municipal Committee, Shanghai Municipal People's Government, and Shanghai Office of the Chinese Academy of Sciences jointly established SUST. Zhou Ren was appointed President. Liu Fang was appointed Deputy Secretary of the Party Committee and Vice President. The first opening ceremony was held in September, 1958.

1959年5月，中国科学院院长郭沫若为学校题写校名
The name of SUST, inscribed by Guo Moruo, President of the Chinese Academy of Sciences, May 1959

校长周仁在 1959 级新生开学典礼上讲话
President Zhou Ren addressing the opening ceremony of the new school year, 1959

1989 年 5 月 19 日，举行庆祝建校 30 周年大会（注：据 2004 年编印的《上海科学技术大学志（1958—1994）》的记载）
Celebration of the 30th anniversary of SUST, May 19, 1989

2. 校园变迁　Relocations of Campuses

1959年5月，临时校址从中国科学院上海分院搬至欧阳路221号（光华大学旧址，校舍与上海机电设计院合用）
The temporary campus of SUST moved to No. 221 Ouyang Road in May 1959.

1964年前，嘉定校园校门（位于学生第一宿舍南侧）
The gate of SUST in Jiading before 1964

学生们欢快地搬入新校园
Students moving to the new campus happily

1960年，迁入嘉定县城中路20号校园（摄于20世纪80年代）
The campus of SUST moved to No. 20 Chengzhong Road, Jiading in 1960. (photo taken in the 1980s)

建于1960年的第一教学楼和建于1985年的校标雕塑（寓意办学目标：培养"高、精、尖"人才）
No. 1 Teaching Building built in 1960 and the sculpture of the university logo set up in 1985

宿舍楼（1960 年建）
The dormitory building (built in 1960)

化学系实验教学楼（1961 年建）
The lab building of the Chemistry Department (built in 1961)

无线电电子学系实验教学楼（1966 年建）
The lab building of the Radio Electronics Department (built in 1966)

3. 学校领导　Leaders of SUST

历任校党委负责人一览
Party Committee Leaders

职　务	姓　名	任职年月
党委书记	刘　芳（副）	1959.9—1965.7
	刘　芳	1965.7—1973
核心小组组长	徐冠彬	1971.5—1973.5
党委书记	马林正	1973.7—1977.10
	张远达	1977.10—1984.2
	沈　冶	1984.2—1986.9
	吴程里（副）	1986.9—1988.9
	吴程里	1988.9—1992.6

历任校长一览
Presidents

职　务	姓　名	任职年月
校长	周　仁	1959.9—（1973.12 去世）
	杨士法	1978.7—1984.3
	金柱青	1984.3—1987.3
	郭本瑜	1987.3—1994.5
名誉校长	严东生	1984.3—1994.5
	黄宏嘉	1987.3—1994.5

首任校长周仁
Zhou Ren, first President of SUST

周仁（1892.8.5—1973.12.3），江苏南京人。冶金学家和陶瓷学家，中国钢铁冶金学、陶瓷学的开创者和奠基人之一，1955年当选为中国科学院学部委员（院士）。1910年毕业于江南高等学堂，同年赴美国康奈尔大学机械工程系求学。1915年获硕士学位，当年回国。曾任南京高等师范学校教授、上海交通大学教务长、中央大学工学院院长。1928年在上海创建中央研究院工程研究所。新中国成立后，历任中国科学院工学实验馆馆长、上海冶金陶瓷研究所所长、上海冶金研究所所长、上海硅酸盐化学与工学研究所所长、中国科学院上海分院副院长等职。中国早期学术刊物和学术团体的创始人之一。

1915年与任鸿隽、赵元任、秉志、杨杏佛、胡明复等人在康奈尔大学创办了中国最早的综合性学术刊物——《科学》，并成立了中国最早的科学社。1933年创办的综合性科普期刊——《科学画刊》，至今仍在发行。

Zhou Ren (August 5, 1892-December 3, 1973) was a metallurgist and ceramist, one of the pioneers and founders of Chinese iron and steel metallurgy and ceramics, and academician of the Chinese Academy of Sciences. He got his master's degree in mechanical engineering from Cornell University in 1915. He served as Provost of Shanghai Jiao Tong University, President of National Central College, and Deputy Dean of the Chinese Academy of Sciences Shanghai Branch. He founded the earliest Chinese academic journal *Science* in Cornell University in 1915 and established the earliest academy of sciences in China.

（二）发展
Development

1. 院市共建　Joint Efforts of Shanghai Government and the Chinese Academy of Sciences

中共上海市委决定，上海科学技术大学筹建工作由上海市副市长兼中国科学院上海办事处主任刘述周负责，中国科学院上海办事处（上海分院）主办，市委、市人委相关部、委、办、局协同合作。中国科学院上海办事处确定了"全院办校，所系结合，分头包干"的建校方案。

Liu Shuzhou, Vice Mayor of Shanghai and Director of Shanghai Office of the Chinese Academy of Sciences, was appointed to lead the preparatory work of SUST, coordinating all the related parties.

建校初期各系主任一览
Chairs of Early Departments

系　别	主　任	中国科学院任职	备　注
技术物理	谢希德	上海技术物理研究所所长	1980年当选中科院学部委员
化学冶金与物理冶金	万　钧	上海冶金研究所党委书记、副所长	
化学冶金与物理冶金	邹元爔（副主任）	上海冶金研究所研究员	1980年当选中科院学部委员
硅酸盐化学与工学	严东生	上海硅酸盐研究所副所长	1980年当选中科院学部委员，1994年当选工程院院士
元素有机化学	汪　猷	上海有机化学研究所副所长	1955年当选中科院学部委员
元素有机化学	黄耀曾（副主任）	上海有机化学研究所研究员	
生物物理化学	王应睐	上海生物化学研究所所长	1955年当选中科院学部委员
生物物理化学	沈昭文（副主任）	上海生物化学研究所研究员	
工程力学	王希季	上海机电设计院总工程师	1993年当选中科院院士，"两弹一星功勋奖章"荣获者
计算数学	李　珩	上海天文台台长	
自动化	胡汝鼎		上海市机电一局原副局长
无线电电子学	毛启爽		上海市市内电话局原副局长

1959年11月,校长周仁主持第一届校务委员会第一次会议,确定办学宗旨和建校方案

President Zhou Ren presiding over the first meeting of the First Council of SUST, November 1959

严东生,1959年5月负责筹建硅酸盐化学与工学系并任系主任,1984—1994年任名誉校长

Yan Dongsheng led the preparation work for the Silicate Chemistry and Engineering Department and served as Chair of the department in 1959. He served as Honorary President of SUST from 1984 to 1994.

建校初期,校党委副书记兼副校长刘芳(中)和生物物理化学系主任王应睐(左二)、系副主任沈昭文(左一)及马瑞德教授(右二)等商量学校工作

Liu Fang, Vice President and Deputy Secretary of the Party Committee (middle), Wang Yinglai, Chair of the Biology, Physics, and Chemistry Department (second from left), Shen Zhaowen, Deputy Chair (first from left), and Professor Ma Ruide (second from right) discussing the university construction

建校初期，硅酸盐化学与工学系主任严东生（右二）、化学冶金与物理冶金系副主任邹元燨（右三）讨论专业方向和教学计划

Yan Dongsheng (second from right), Chair of the Silicate Chemistry and Engineering Department, and Zou Yuanxi (third from right), Deputy Chair of the Chemical Metallurgy and Physical Metallurgy Department, discussing the disciplinary programs and teaching plans

建校初期，刘芳（中）和副教务长兼无线电电子系主任毛启爽（右二）、副教务长兼自动化系主任胡汝鼎（左二）等人讨论专业方向和教学计划

Liu Fang (middle), President and Deputy Secretary of the Party Committee, Mao Qishuang (second from right), Deputy Provost and Chair of the Radio Electronics Department, and Hu Ruding (second from left), Deputy Provost and Chair of the Automation Department, discussing the disciplinary programs and teaching plans

建校初期，中国科学院上海一些研究所负责人正在研究上海科学技术大学教学计划（右起：上海植物生理研究所所长殷宏章、上海生理研究所所长冯德培、上海生物化学研究所所长王应睐、上海生物化学研究所研究员沈昭文）

Directors from the related research institutes of the Chinese Academy of Sciences in Shanghai discussing the teaching plans of SUST

2. 上级关心　Visits of Leaders

1961年10月，中共上海市委书记处候补书记、上海市副市长兼中国科学院上海分院院长刘述周（中）来校视察，观看嘉定校园建设规划沙盘

Liu Shuzhou (middle), Alternate Secretary of the Secretariat of the CPC Shanghai Municipal Committee, Vice Mayor of Shanghai, and President of the Chinese Academy of Sciences Shanghai Branch, inspecting SUST, October 1961

1963年，中共上海市委书记处候补书记兼教卫部部长杨西光来校视察

Yang Xiguang, Alternate Secretary of the Secretariat of the CPC Shanghai Municipal Committee and Minister of Education and Health, visiting SUST, 1963

1985年10月，中共上海市委副书记黄菊来校视察（前排左二起：校党委书记沈㤗、黄菊、上海市副市长刘振元、中共上海市教卫工作党委副书记胡绿漪）

Huang Ju, Deputy Secretary of the CPC Shanghai Municipal Committee, inspecting SUST, October 1985 (from second on the left in the first row: Shen Yi, Secretary of the Party Committee of SUST, Huang Ju, Liu Zhenyuan, Vice Mayor of Shanghai, and Hu Lüyi, Deputy Secretary of the CPC Committee of Shanghai Municipal Education and Health Work)

1990年4月，中共上海市委副书记吴邦国（左三）来校视察

Wu Bangguo (third from left), Deputy Secretary of the CPC Shanghai Municipal Committee, inspecting SUST, April 1990

3. 人才培养　Talent Cultivation

1988年，召开学生思想政治工作研讨会（左起：校党委副书记林玉凤、校长郭本瑜、校党委书记吴程里）

Seminar on students cultivation, 1988 (from left to right: Deputy Secretary of the Party Committee Lin Yufeng, President Guo Benyu, and Secretary of the Party Committee Wu Chengli)

1963年，学生在学习《毛泽东选集》
Students studying *Selected Works of Mao Zedong*, 1963

第二部分　1958—1994 年的"四校"　　　　　　　　二、上海科学技术大学

建校初期，副教务长兼自动化系主任胡汝鼎教授在指导学生
Professor Hu Ruding, Deputy Provost and Chair of the Automation Department, instructing students

建校初期，数学系黄育仁教授在指导学生
Huang Yuren, a professor of the Department of Mathematics, instructing students

1975 年，精密机械工程系青年教师王生洪（后排右三）在指导学生毕业设计
Wang Shenghong (third from right in the back row), a young teacher of the Department of Precision Mechanical Engineering, instructing students on their graduation project, 1975

1981年，电磁场与微波技术专业获得博士学位授予权，成为学校第一个博士点。图为博士生导师黄宏嘉院士（中）在主持研究生答辩

Professor and Academician Huang Hongjia (middle) presiding over a dissertation defense, 1981

无线电物理与无线电电子学专业博士生导师鲍家善教授在指导青年教师

Bao Jiashan, a doctoral supervisor of radio physics and electronics, instructing a young teacher

计算数学专业博士生导师郭本瑜教授（中）在指导研究生

Guo Benyu (middle), a doctoral supervisor of Computing Mathematics, instructing graduate students

运筹学与控制论专业博士生导师郑权教授在指导研究生

Zheng Quan, a doctoral supervisor of Operations Research and Cybernetics, instructing a graduate student

1981年，首届研究生毕业，与导师合影
Graduation photo of the first batch of graduate students with supervisors, 1981

1960年6月，中共上海市委批转上海科学技术大学关于招收工人班的请示批复
The Proposal Report on admission of excellent workers to SUST, June 1960

1960年9月，中共上海市委书记处候补书记、副市长刘述周来校作报告，强调招收工人班的意义
Liu Shuzhou, Alternate Secretary of the Secretariat of the CPC Shanghai Municipal Committee and Vice Mayor of Shanghai, reporting on the significance of recruiting workers at SUST, 1960

1965年，工人班首届毕业生、全国著名劳动模范王林鹤毕业设计答辩
Wang Linhe, a student of the first Worker Class and National Model Worker, defending his graduation dissertation, 1965

4. 科学研究　Scientific Research

科学研究成果获国家级奖项一览
National Awards and Achievements

科研项目	奖项名称	等级	年度	获奖人
耦合模式理论研究	全国科学大会"重大贡献奖"		1978	黄宏嘉
流体力学中的差分方法	全国科学大会"优秀科研成果奖"		1978	郭本瑜
红旗渠潜水泵的密封材料	全国科学大会"优秀科研成果奖"		1978	周积春　刘文义
膦肼叶立德在合成含氟有机化合物中应用的研究	国家自然科学奖	三等奖	1982	丁维钰
建立国家激光洛氏硬度和表面洛氏硬度基准主测量系统	国家科技进步奖	二等奖	1985	陈明仪　陈久康　孙桂清　王菊荣
模式耦合理论及其在微波和光传输中的应用	国家自然科学奖	二等奖	1987	黄宏嘉
微波介质谐振器材料——A6陶瓷	国家发明奖	三等奖	1987	方永汉　胡昂
高精度20米口径卫星地面站天线系统	国家科技进步奖	一等奖	1987	王生洪　龚振邦　吴家麟　郭锡章
辐射合成超薄型亲水软接触镜	国家发明奖	二等奖	1988	刘钰铭　杨月琪　阮逸标
氘氚化锂制造技术	国家发明奖	二等奖	1988	毕清华
单模光纤技术	国家科技进步奖	二等奖	1988	黄宏嘉
熔锥型单模光纤无源器件的制造技术与装置	国家发明奖	三等奖	1990	汪道刚
非线性偏微分方程的差分方法和谱方法及其应用	国家教委科技进步奖	一等奖	1990	郭本瑜　马和平　曹伟明

黄宏嘉院士是我国单模光纤技术的开拓者，他的"耦合模式理论研究"在 1978 年获全国科学大会"重大贡献奖"，"模式耦合理论及其在微波和光传输中的应用"获 1987 年国家自然科学奖二等奖，"单模光纤技术"获 1988 年国家科技进步二等奖。

Academician Huang Hongjia is a pioneer of the single-mode optical fiber technology in China. His "Research on Coupling Mode" was awarded Significant Contribution Award in the 1978 National Science Conference, "Mode Coupling Theory and Its Application in Microwave and Optical Transmission" the Second Prize of the 1987 National Natural Science Award, and "Single-Mode Optical Fiber Technology" the Second Prize of the 1988 National Prize for Progress in Science and Technology.

黄宏嘉（左）1980 年主持研制出我国第一根单模光纤

Huang Hongjia (left) presiding over the development of China's first single-mode optical fiber, 1980

黄宏嘉 1963 年出版的《微波原理》是国内在该领域的第一本专著，被国际学界称作是一本"为中国人争气的书"

Huang Hongjia's *Microwave Principles*, published in 1963, is the first monograph in the field of microwave theory in China and a book enjoying international recognition.

由丁维钰教授（右）主持、与中国科学院上海有机化学研究所合作完成的"膦胂叶立德在合成含氟有机化合物中应用的研究"获1982年度国家自然科学奖三等奖

The project "Study on the Application of Organophosphorus and Organoarsenic Ylides in the Synthesis of Fluoroorganic Compounds" in cooperation with Shanghai Organic Institute of the Chinese Academy of Sciences, directed by Professor Ding Weiyu (right), winning the Third Prize of the 1982 National Natural Science Award

由王生洪教授（中）主持、与中国人民解放军总参谋部第五十七研究所合作完成的"高精度20米口径卫星地面站天线系统"获1987年度国家科技进步奖一等奖

The project "The Ground Station Antenna System of High-Precision 20-meter Satellite" in collaboration with the No. 57 Institute of PLA General Staff Department, directed by Professor Wang Shenghong (middle), winning the First Prize of the 1987 National Prize for Progress in Science and Technology

陈明仪教授主持的"建立国家激光洛氏硬度和表面洛氏硬度基准主测量系统"获1985年度国家科技进步奖二等奖

The project "Establishment of National Laser Rockwell Scale and Surface Rockwell Scale Benchmark Measurement System," directed by Professor Chen Mingyi, winning the Second Prize of the 1985 National Prize for Progress in Science and Technology

方永汉、胡昂的"微波介质谐振器材料——A6陶瓷"获1987年度国家发明奖三等奖

The project "The Material of Microwave Dielectric Resonator-A6 Ceramic," co-directed by Fang Yonghan and Hu Ang, winning the Third Prize of the 1987 National Invention Award

刘钰铭教授（中）主持的"辐射合成超薄型亲水软接触镜"获1988年度国家发明奖二等奖

The project "Ultrathin Hydrophilic Soft Contact Lenses Synthesized by Radiation," directed by Professor Liu Yuming (middle), winning the Second Prize of the 1988 National Invention Award

毕清华研究员的"氘氚化锂制造技术"获1988年度国家发明奖二等奖

The project "Manufacturing Technology for Lithium Deuterium Tritide," directed by Researcher Bi Qinghua, winning the Second Prize of the 1988 National Invention Award

汪道刚教授的"熔锥型单模光纤无源器件的制造技术与装置"获1990年度国家发明奖三等奖

The project "Manufacturing Technology and Devices of Non-original Devices of Fused-Tapered Single-Mode Optical Fiber," directed by Professor Wang Daogang, winning the Third Prize of the 1990 National Invention Award

郭本瑜教授主持的"非线性偏微分方程的差分方法和谱方法及其应用"获1990年度国家教委科技进步奖一等奖

The project "Differential Method and Spectral Method of Nonlinear Differential Equation and Its Application," directed by Professor Guo Benyu, winning the First Prize of the 1990 Science and Technology Progress Award of the National Education Commission

1980年10月，中国物理学会、核学会粒子加速器学会成立大会暨学术交流会在上海科学技术大学举行

The Founding Conference of the Chinese Physical Society and the Nuclear Accelerator Society at SUST, October 1980

5. 国际交流　International Exchanges

1985—1991年，联合国原子能机构委托上海科学技术大学射线应用研究所先后举办了三期亚太地区辐射交联技术培训班。图为第一期培训班成员合影（前排左四：上海科学技术大学射线应用研究所马瑞德教授，前排右一：研究所周慕尧副研究员）

The group photo of trainees of the first training program on radiation technology (Professor Ma Ruide of SUST, fourth from left in the front row; Associate Researcher Zhou Muyao, first from right in the front row). From 1985 to 1991, the United Nations Atomic Energy Agency entrusted the Institute of Radiation Application of SUST to hold three training programs for trainees from Asian Pacific areas.

1987年，日本鲭江市日中友好协会会长、上海科学技术大学顾问教授山本治（左二）资助上海科学技术大学举办日语进修班、汉语培训班及建造"谊园"宾馆签约仪式在校内举行，副校长孙生官（右二）代表学校签字

Agreement signing ceremony attended by Vice President Sun Shengguan (second from right) and Osamu Yamamoto (second from left), President of the Japan-China Friendship Association of Sabae City and SUST Consultant Professor, 1987

1988年，被国家教委列为用英语教学招收外国来华留学博士生的首批试点单位之一。图为首届巴基斯坦来华留学生博士论文答辩（前排左二起：上海科学技术大学黄宏嘉院士、电子科技大学谢处方教授、上海科学技术大学鲍家善教授和徐得名教授）

Professors attending the doctoral dissertation defense of the first Pakistani student (from second on the left in the front row: Academician Huang Hongjia from SUST, Professor Xie Chufang from University of Electronic Science and Technology, and Professor Bao Jiashan and Professor Xu Deming from SUST). In 1988, SUST was listed by the National Education Commission as one of the first pilot units to recruit English-taught overseas doctoral students.

1988年，校长郭本瑜和校党委书记吴程里会见到访的欧共体访华代表团

President Guo Benyu and Secretary of the Party Committee Wu Chengli receiving the visiting delegation of the European Communities, 1988

1990年，副校长徐得名（左三）和到访的外国同行在学校光纤通信实验室探讨科学问题
Vice President Xu Deming (third from left) and visiting scholars discussing scientific issues in the optical fiber communication laboratory, 1990

1991年，举行聘请外籍专家为学校名誉教授暨国外大学授予黄宏嘉院士为名誉博士的授证仪式
Certificate awarding ceremony, 1991. Professor W. A. Gambling was employed as honorary professor of SUST and Academician Huang Hongjia was conferred an honorary DSc degree by the Eurotech, Hawaii.

1991年，与德国汉堡哈尔堡工业大学签订文化教育科技合作协议书
Cooperation agreement signing ceremony between SUST and Hamburg University of Technology, 1991

1991年，校长郭本瑜主持"上海市—法国罗纳·阿尔卑斯大区双边光纤科学技术研讨会"
President Guo Benyu presiding over the "Shanghai-France Rhône-Alpes Bilateral Optical Fiber Science and Technology Seminar," 1991

1992年，校党委副书记、副校长周慕尧会见到访的国际原子能机构代表

Zhou Muyao, Deputy Secretary of the Party Committee and Vice President of SUST, talking with the visiting representative of the International Atomic Energy Agency, 1992

获全国荣誉称号人员
Faculty Winning National Honors

荣誉称号	年　度	姓　名
全国"五一"劳动奖章	1986	周幼威
全国"五一"劳动奖章	1993	王保华
全国教育系统劳动模范	1986	邵　俊
全国优秀教师	1989	龚振邦
全国优秀教师	1989	郭本瑜
全国优秀教师	1991	王保华
全国优秀教师	1991	王德人
全国优秀教师	1993	陈体芳
全国优秀教师	1993	陈久康

上海大学
Shanghai University

（一）创建
Re-foundation

1. 学校成立　Re-founding of SHU

　　1959年，上海市美术学校成立；1978年，复旦大学分校、华东师范大学仪表电子分校、上海科学技术大学分校、上海外国语学院分院、上海机械学院轻工分院相继成立。1985年，上海法律专科学校成立，并于1992年改名为上海法律高等专科学校。

　　1983年5月，教育部批准上述5所分校（院）和上海市美术学校合并组建为上海大学，随后，上海市政府教卫办组建学校筹建组；7月，上海市政府同意市教卫办关于筹建上海大学的意见；9月，上海大学新生开学。

　　1993年，上海法律高等专科学校并入上海大学。截至1994年4月，上海大学设有文学院、工学院、国际商学院、美术学院和法学院。

　　In 1959, Shanghai Fine Arts College was founded. In 1978, branches of Fudan University, SUST, Shanghai Foreign Language Institute, Shanghai Light Industry Machinery College, and Instrumentation, Electronics Campus of East China Normal University were founded.

　　In May 1983, the Ministry of Education approved the combining of the above five branches and Shanghai Fine Arts College to form SHU. In July, Shanghai Municipal People's Government approved the re-establishment of SHU. In September, the freshmen of SHU began their new term.

　　In 1993, Shanghai Law College was merged into SHU. By April 1994, SHU had set up five colleges in liberal arts, engineering, international business, fine arts, and law.

1983年，北京大学教授、老上海大学（1922—1927年的上海大学）教员俞平伯为上海大学题词

An inscription for SHU by Yu Pingbo, a professor of Peking University and faculty member of SHU (1922-1927), 1983

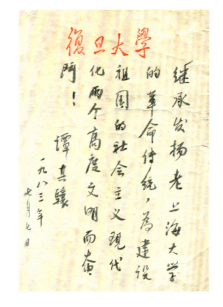

1983年，复旦大学教授、老上海大学学生谭其骧为上海大学题词

An inscription for SHU by Tan Qixiang, a professor of Fudan University and student of SHU (1922-1927), 1983

第二部分　1958—1994年的"四校"　　　　　　　　　　　　　　　　　　　　　　　　　　三、上海大学

上海市政府在同意市教卫办关于筹建上海大学的意见中要求："上海大学要在教育改革的试验中，不断总结经验，提高教学质量。"

Feedback from Shanghai Municipal People's Government, saying "SHU should constantly accumulate experience and improve the quality of teaching in the educational reform"

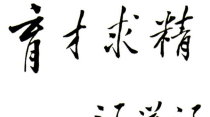

1983年8月，上海市市长汪道涵为上海大学题词

An inscription for SHU by Wang Daohan, Mayor of Shanghai, August 1983

1985年5月，确定上海大学校标，图中一棵发芽的枯树，寓意上海大学成立恰似老上海大学枯木逢春，六个枝叶代表上海大学由六所学校合并组建而成

The logo of SHU created in May 1985, picturing a withered tree sprouting with six branches of leaves, signifying a revitalized SHU combined with six branches of colleges and institutes

1985年11月，中央军委副主席、老上海大学学生杨尚昆为上海大学题词

An inscription for SHU by Yang Shangkun, Vice Chairman of the Central Military Commission and student of SHU (1922-1927), November 1985

2. 校园变迁   Relocations of Campuses

1983年，位于上海市凯旋路30号的
上海大学（校部所在地）
SHU at No. 30 Kaixuan Road, 1983

1987年，位于上海市新闸路1220号的上海大学（校部所在地）
SHU at No. 1220 Xinzha Road, 1987

位于上海市外青松公路7989号的法学院
The Law School at No. 7989 Waiqingsong Road

1983年，位于上海市西江湾路547号的文学院
The College of Liberal Arts at No. 547 West Jiangwan Road, 1983

1990年2月，文学院迁至上海市三门路661号
The College of Liberal Arts at No. 661 Sanmen Road, February 1990

位于上海市中山南二路 600 号的工学院

The College of Engineering at No. 600 Second South Zhongshan Road

位于上海市蒲西路 150 号的外国语学院

The School of Foreign Languages at No. 150 Puxi Road

位于上海市新闸路 1220 号的工商管理学院

The College of Business Administration at No. 1220 Xinzha Road

1985 年，外国语学院改名为国际商业学院；1986 年 4 月，工商管理学院改名为商学院；1993 年 9 月，两个学院合并为国际商学院，并搬至新校区——上海市莲花路 211 号。图为正在建设中的莲花路校区

The campus under construction at No. 211 Lianhua Road. In 1985, the School of Foreign Languages was renamed the College of International Business. In April 1986, the College of Business Administration was renamed Business School. In September 1993, the two colleges merged into the School of International Business and moved to the new campus at No. 211 Lianhua Road.

1959年，上海市美术学校成立；1960年9月上海市美术专科学校（五年制本科）成立；1983年5月并入上海大学，成为上海大学美术学院。

In 1959, Shanghai Fine Arts College was established. In September 1960, Shanghai Academy of Fine Arts (five-year undergraduate program) was established. In May 1983, it was merged into SHU and became SHU Academy of Fine Arts.

1960年，位于上海市陕西北路500号（原西摩会堂——犹太人教堂）的上海市美术专科学校
Shanghai Academy of Fine Arts at No. 500 North Shaanxi Road, 1960

1983年，位于上海市凯旋路30号的美术学院
SHU Academy of Fine Arts at No. 30 Kaixuan Road, 1983

3. 学校领导　Leaders of SHU

校党委书记及历任校长一览
Secretary of the Party Committee and Presidents

职　务	姓　名	任职年月
党委书记	孟宪勤	1984.4—1993.10
校长	王生洪（兼）	1987.5—1993.1
	杨德广	1993.1—1994.5

（注：王生洪时任上海市政府教卫办主任兼高教局局长）

1984年，校领导合影（左起：副校长曹仲贤、主持工作的副校长杜信恩、校党委书记孟宪勤、校党委副书记盛善珠）
Some SHU leaders in 1984 (from left to right: Vice President Cao Zhongxian, Executive Vice President Du Xin'en, Secretary of the Party Committee Meng Xianqin, and Deputy Secretary Sheng Shanzhu)

1993年1月，校领导班子欢迎杨德广校长到任（左起：副校长李明忠、副校长曹仲贤、校党委副书记盛善珠、杨德广、王生洪、校党委书记孟宪勤、副校长林炯如）
SHU leaders welcoming new President Yang Deguang, January 1993 (from left to right: Vice President Li Mingzhong, Vice President Cao Zhongxian, Deputy Secretary of the Party Committee Sheng Shanzhu, President Yang Deguang, Former President Wang Shenghong, Secretary of the Party Committee Meng Xianqin, and Vice President Lin Jiongru)

4. 上级关心　Support of Leaders

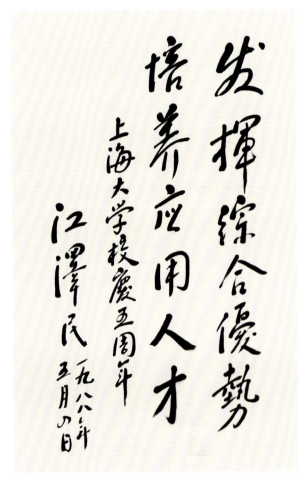

1988年5月，中共中央政治局委员、上海市委书记江泽民为上海大学题词

An inscription for SHU by Jiang Zemin, Secretary of the CPC Shanghai Municipal Committee, May 1988

1992年3月，国家教委副主任朱开轩（左二）视察上海大学

Zhu Kaixuan (second from left), Deputy Director of the National Education Commission, inspecting SHU, March 1992

（二）发展
Development

1. 人才培养与科学研究　Talent Cultivation and Scientific Research

1984年10月，教育部批复同意授予费孝通教授为上海大学名誉教授。图为1983年12月，费孝通教授在上海大学文学院作学术报告
Professor Fei Xiaotong lecturing at the College of Liberal Arts at SHU, October 1984

1994年1月，召开校务委员会第一次会议
The first meeting of the University Council, January 1994

1994年2月，上海工业大学钱伟长校长访问上海大学法学院

President of SUT Qian Weichang visiting the Law School of SHU, February 1994

1994年4月，上海工业大学钱伟长校长由上海工业大学党委书记吴程里（右二）陪同访问上海大学工学院

President of SUT Qian Weichang visiting the School of Engineering of SHU, April 1994

在李庆云（左一，文学院首任党委书记）的推动下，文学院前身复旦大学分校建立了"文革"以后第一个社会学系，使学校成为全国最早恢复社会学专业教学的高校

Li Qingyun (first from left, the first Secretary of the Party Committee of the College of Liberal Arts), promoting the establishment of the major of sociology, the earliest sociology major re-established in China after the "Cultural Revolution," at Branch of Fudan University, the former College of Liberal Arts

文学院在上海首开"社会学讲习班"

The first "Sociology Workshop" in Shanghai, held by the College of Liberal Arts of SHU

文学院前身复旦大学分校于1981年创办的《社会》杂志是国内最早公开发行的社会学专业期刊（右图为创刊号封面）

The first issue of *Sociology*, the first academic journal of the discipline in China, started by Branch of Fudan University, the former College of Liberal Arts of SHU, 1981

文学院于 1983 年创办的《秘书》杂志是国内最早公开发行的秘书学专业期刊（右图为创刊号封面）

The first issue of *Secretary*, the first academic journal of the discipline in China, started by the College of Liberal Arts of SHU, 1983

文学院院长王熙梅教授在进行国家社科"八五"规划重点项目研究

Professor Wang Ximei, Dean of the College of Liberal Arts, working on a national key project

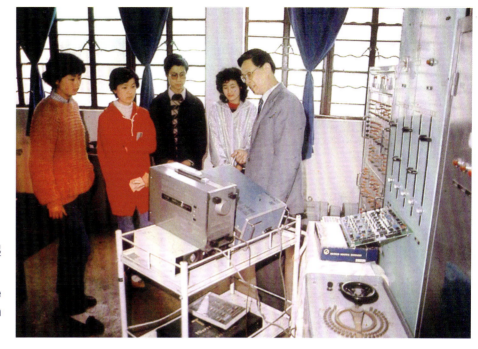

工学院院长马国琳教授（右一）与教师一起开展教学研究

Professor Ma Guolin (first from right), Dean of the School of Engineering, conducting teaching research with colleagues

工学院院长陈大森教授在指导学生做实验

Professor Chen Dasen, Dean of the School of Engineering, instructing students on their experiments

与上海市财政局合办世界银行贷款项目评估培训班
The opening ceremony of the World Bank Loan Project Evaluation Training Program, co-organized with Shanghai Finance Bureau

国际商学院院长唐豪教授在授课
Professor Tang Hao, Dean of the School of International Business, lecturing to the students

国际商业学院与上海航头商城签订"航头商城奖励基金协议书"
Agreement signing ceremony between the College of International Business and Shanghai Hangtou Mall

第二部分　1958—1994年的"四校"　　　　　　　　　　　　　　三、上海大学

国际商学院学生到美国的商务机构实习
Intern students from the School of International Business at a business organization in the United States

法学院学生开设模拟法庭
Students from the Law School at a mock court trial

美术学院学生到街上美化环境
Students from the Academy of Fine Arts painting on the street

上海市美术专科学校创建者
Founders of Shanghai Academy of Fine Arts

沈之瑜（1916—1990），1960年任副校长（不设正校长）兼党支部书记

Shen Zhiyu (1916-1990), Vice President and Secretary of the Party Branch of Shanghai Academy of Fine Arts from 1960

涂克（1916—2012），1960年分管油画系、雕塑系

Tu Ke (1916-2012), in charge of the Departments of Oil Painting and Sculpture of Shanghai Academy of Fine Arts from 1960

丁浩（1917—2011），1960年分管国画系、工艺美术系

Ding Hao (1917-2011), in charge of the Department of Traditional Chinese Painting and Art and Crafts of Shanghai Academy of Fine Arts from 1960

张充仁（1907—1998），1960年入职上海市美术专科学校，1962年任雕塑研究室主任

Zhang Chongren (1907-1998), entering Shanghai Academy of Fine Arts in 1960 and serving as Director of Sculpture Research Office from 1962

孟光（1921—1996），1962年任素描专修科班主任，1979年任上海市美术学校副校长

Meng Guang (1921-1996), Chair of the Sketching Class of Shanghai Academy of Fine Arts from 1962 and Vice President of Shanghai Fine Arts College from 1979

张雪父（1911—1987），1960年入职上海市美术专科学校，1978年任上海市美术学校校长

Zhang Xuefu (1911-1987), entering Shanghai Academy of Fine Arts in 1960 and serving as President of Shanghai Fine Arts College from 1978

上海大学美术学院创建者
Founders of SHU Academy of Fine Arts

李天祥（1928—2020），
1985年任院长
Li Tianxiang (1928-2020), Dean of SHU Academy of Fine Arts from 1985

任意（1925—1998），
1984年任副院长
Ren Yi (1925-1998), Deputy Dean of SHU Academy of Fine Arts from 1984

张自申（1933— ），
1984年任副院长
Zhang Zishen (1933-), Deputy Dean of SHU Academy of Fine Arts from 1984

顾炳鑫（1923—2001），
1985年任国画系主任
Gu Bingxin (1923-2001), Chair of the Department of Traditional Chinese Painting at SHU Academy of Fine Arts from 1985

廖炯模（1932—2020），
1985年任油画系主任
Liao Jiongmo (1932-2020), Chair of the Department of Oil Painting at SHU Academy of Fine Arts from 1985

章永浩（1933— ），
1986年任雕塑系主任
Zhang Yonghao (1933-), Chair of the Department of Sculpture at SHU Academy of Fine Arts from 1986

曹有成（1929— ），
1985年任中专部主任
Cao Youcheng (1929-), Chair of the Vocational Division at SHU Academy of Fine Arts from 1985

韩和平（1932—2019），
1988年任美术研究所主任
Han Heping (1932-2019), Chair of the Institute of Fine Arts, SHU Academy of Fine Arts from 1988

1965年，上海市美术专科学校 1960 级毕业生与全体教师合影

Graduation photo of the teachers and the Class of 1965 of Shanghai Academy of Fine Arts, 1965

文化艺术创作优秀作品一览
Outstanding Works and Awards

作品名称	获得荣誉	年 度	作 者
《列宁全集》第二版第五十三卷（译著）	中共中央宣传部、中央编译局著作奖	1989	张 坚
《公共关系心理学》（专著）	第二届全国金钥匙奖三等奖	1990	周振明
《档案文献保护技术》（专著）	全国"七五"优秀论著三等奖	1990	宋善玲 等
《中国历代帝王录》（专著）	上海市十佳著作	1990	杨剑宇
《李心传著作编年》（专著）	全国古籍图书优秀奖	1991	来可泓
《大学德育论》（专著）	上海市1968—1993年社会科学优秀成果三等奖	1993	杨德广
"陈毅"（雕塑）	耸立在上海外滩	1990	章永浩
"上海市人民英雄纪念塔"（雕塑）	耸立在上海外滩公园	1989	张海平 等
"升"（雕塑）	耸立在美国纽约联合国大厦前草坪	1990	吴慧明
"飞虹"（雕塑）	耸立在上海虹桥国际机场	1992	张海平
"军魂"（雕塑）	耸立在上海高桥烈士陵园	1997	张海平
"澜沧江畔"（国画）	第六届全国美术作品展优秀作品奖	1984	应野平
"大森林"（油画）	全国美术作品展一等奖		李天祥
"苏醒"（油画）	第六届全国美术作品展优秀作品奖	1984	李天祥
"书林"（封面装帧）	全国期刊封面评选一等奖	1985	任 意
"走出草地"（油画）	全军美术作品展优秀奖	1987	张自申
"漆画"	第七届全国美术作品展银奖	1989	葛春学
"不染"（国画）	第七届全国美术作品展银奖	1989	陈家泠
"残雪"（油画）	第七届全国美术作品展铜奖	1989	凌启宁
"少女"（雕塑）	第七届全国美术作品展作品奖	1989	杨剑平

(续表)

作品名称	获得荣誉	年度	作者
"猫头鹰"（摄影）	"彩色世界"全国摄影大奖赛二等奖		庄小蔚
"中国历代服饰"（装帧设计）	莱比锡国际书籍装帧艺术展铜奖	1989	任 意
"土巷"（油画）	第十二届国际美术作品展荣誉奖		廖炯模
"插图"	联合国教科文组织颁发世界儿童读物插图奖		姜明立
"白求恩"（雕塑）	建党70周年全国美术作品展铜奖	1991	张海平
"中国共产党的亲密战友——宋庆龄"（雕塑）	建党70周年全国美术作品展铜奖	1991	唐锐鹤
"中共一大的一员虎将和一位学者——李达"（油画）	建党70周年全国美术作品展银奖	1991	章德明
"蓝天"（油画）	纪念毛泽东同志《在延安文艺座谈会上的讲话》发表50周年全国美术作品展创作奖	1992	步欣农
"我奶奶和我爸爸"（雕塑）	纪念毛泽东同志《在延安文艺座谈会上的讲话》发表50周年全国美术作品展铜奖	1992	徐韵新
"周恩来总理"（雕塑）	中国美术馆收藏		章永浩
"陈毅副总理"（雕塑）	中国美术馆收藏		章永浩
"散步"（雕塑）	中国美术馆收藏		唐锐鹤
"演员"（雕塑）	中国美术馆收藏		唐锐鹤
"银枪闪烁"（雕塑）	瑞士国际奥林匹克博物馆		张海平
"深壑"（油画）	日本京都博物馆收藏	1986	张自申
"强渡天堑"（油画）	中国人民革命军事博物馆收藏	1987	张自申
"树"（油画）	美国亚洲太平洋博物馆收藏	1989	王劼音
"门楼"（版画）	法国国家博物馆收藏	1990	王劼音
"祖国的明珠——宝钢"（油画）	中国油画馆收藏	1991	廖炯模
"壁画"10幅	北京人民大会堂收藏	1992	郭 力 等
"望气"（版画）3幅	澳大利亚南威尔士国家博物馆收藏	1992	王劼音

2. 国际交流　International Exchanges

1986年，国际商业学院院长卢关泉（右一）参加国际高级经理班毕业典礼
Lu Guanquan (first from right), Dean of the College of International Business, at the graduation ceremony of International Senior Management Class, 1986

1986年，工商管理学院院长蒋嘉俊（左）在校会见来访的外宾
Jiang Jiajun (left), Dean of the College of Business Administration, talking with visiting guests, 1986

1986年，副校长杜信恩（右）、美术学院院长李天祥（中）和德国柏林艺术高等学校校长乌罗明出席两校校际交流签字仪式
Exchange agreement signing ceremony between Berlin University of the Arts and SHU Academy of Fine Arts, 1986 (from left to right: Ulrich Roloff-Momin, President of Berlin University of the Arts, Li Tianxiang, Dean of SHU Academy of Fine Arts, and Du Xin'en, Vice President of SHU)

1986年，与日本大阪艺术大学签订交流协议书
Exchange agreement signing ceremony with Osaka University of Arts, 1986

1988年，校党委书记孟宪勤（左）在美术学院会见参加中日交流作品展的日本友人
Secretary of the Party Committee Meng Xianqin (left) meeting with a Japanese visitor at a Sino-Japanese exchange exhibition, 1988

1988年，副校长林炯如在美国纽约市立大学发表演讲

Vice President Lin Jiongru giving a talk at the City University of New York, 1988

1992年，校长王生洪（中）参加日本三城株式会社向工学院赠送光学眼镜仪器交接仪式

President Wang Shenghong (middle) attending a donation ceremony, 1992

1993年，国际商学院举办国际学术研讨会

The international symposium held by the School of International Business, 1993

美术学院外国留学生学习中国画

International students learning Chinese painting at SHU Academy of Fine Arts

获全国荣誉称号人员
Faculty Winning National Honors

荣誉称号	年度	姓名
全国教育系统劳动模范	1989	王宇平
全国优秀教师	1989	王乃樑
全国优秀教师	1989	毛忠明
全国优秀教师	1993	何平立

上海科技高等专科学校
Shanghai College of Science and Technology (SCST)

（一）创建
Foundation

1. 学校成立　Founding of SCST

1959 年 2 月，中共上海市委教卫部决定将复旦中学高中部改制为上海计算技术学校（中专），并决定由教卫部、市科委、中国科学院上海分院以及华东计算技术研究所共同筹建学校；10 月，学校改名为上海第二科学技术学校。1960 年，学校搬至新校区——上海市嘉定县金沙路 280 号。1970—1981 年，学校几度改名；1981 年，学校更名为上海科技专科学校，隶属上海市高教局；1992 年，学校更名为上海科技高等专科学校。

In February 1959, the Education and Health Department of the CPC Shanghai Municipal Committee decided to transform the senior high school division of Fudan High School into Shanghai Computer Technology School. In October, the school was renamed Shanghai Second Science and Technology School. In 1960, it moved to the campus at No. 280 Jinsha Road, Jiading County, Shanghai. In 1981, the school was renamed Shanghai Junior College of Science and Technology. In 1992, it was renamed Shanghai College of Science and Technology.

1959 年，位于上海市华山路 1626 号（复旦中学校舍）的上海计算技术学校校门

The gate of Shanghai Computer Technology School at No. 1626 Huashan Road, 1959

1989 年 5 月 15 日，举行庆祝上海科技专科学校建校 30 周年大会

Celebration of the 30th anniversary of the founding of Shanghai Junior College of Science and Technology, May 15, 1989

第二部分　1958—1994年的"四校"　　　　　　　　　　　　　　　　　　　　　　　　四、上海科技高等专科学校

2. 校园风貌　Views of Campus

教学楼
Teaching buildings

图书馆
The library

3. 学校领导　Leaders of SCST

历任党的负责人一览　Party Committee Leaders

校　名	党组织机构	书　记	任职年月
上海第二科学技术学校	支部	容振华	1959.10—
		杨文林	1961.11—
	总支	杨文林	1964.2—
上海电子专科学校	党委	庄起良	1971.6—
上海市仪表局"七二一"工人大学	党委	陈玉寿（主持）	1977.8—
上海科学技术大学分部	领导小组	桂荣安（组长）	1978.12
	总支	倪美祥	1979.4—
上海科技专科学校	党委	倪美祥	1983.5—
		唐祥庆	1988.7—
		汪国铎	1991.7—
上海科技高等专科学校	党委	沈学超	1993.4—

历任行政负责人一览　Presidents and Directors

校　名	校　长	任职年月
上海第二科学技术学校	胡介峰	1959.10—
上海电子专科学校	杨文林（领导小组组长）	1971.2—
上海市仪表局"七二一"工人大学	庄起良（主任）	1975.8—
上海科学技术大学分部	桂荣安（主任）	1979.4—
上海科技专科学校	桂荣安	1983.6—
	钱孝衡	1984.6—
	潘道才	1987.8—
上海科技高等专科学校	汪国铎	1993.4—

1988年，校党委书记唐祥庆（右）和副书记陆凤鸣
Secretary of the Party Committee Tang Xiangqing (right) and Deputy Secretary Lu Fengming, 1988

1988年，校行政领导合影（左起：校长助理常增庆、副校长刘尚仁、校长潘道才、副校长朱声海）
Administrative leaders, 1988 (from left to right: Assistant President Chang Zengqing, Vice President Liu Shangren, President Pan Daocai, and Vice President Zhu Shenghai)

校领导合影（左起：潘道才、钱孝衡、唐祥庆、忻福良）
Leaders of SCST (from left to right: Pan Daocai, Qian Xiaoheng, Tang Xiangqing, and Xin Fuliang)

1993年，校领导在新校门前合影（左起：党委副书记蒋乃平、党委书记沈学超、校长汪国铎、副校长常增庆）
Leaders of SCST in front of the new gate, 1993 (from left to right: Deputy Secretary of the Party Committee Jiang Naiping, Secretary of the Party Committee Shen Xuechao, President Wang Guoduo, and Vice President Chang Zengqing)

（二）发展
Development

1. 人才培养与科学研究　Talent Cultivation and Scientific Research

计算机技术系主任吴震蒙高级工程师在备课
Senior Engineer Wu Zhenmeng, Chair of the Computer Technology Department, preparing for lessons

电子技术系主任张苹迦副教授（中）在主持系务会议
Associate Professor Zhang Pingjia (middle), Chair of the Department of Electronic Technology, presiding over the department meeting

技术物理系主任薛鸣鹤副教授（右二）和其他系领导商谈工作
Associate Professor Xue Minghe (second from right), Chair of the Department of Technical Physics, discussing with other department leaders

机械技术系主任刘兴东副教授（左一）在指导青年教师
Associate Professor Liu Xingdong (first from left), Chair of the Department of Mechanical Technology, instructing young teachers

第二部分　1958—1994年的"四校"　　　　　　　　　　　　　　　　　　四、上海科技高等专科学校

学生在实验室学习装配电视机

Students learning to assemble TV sets in the laboratory

学生在进行毕业设计答辩

A student at the dissertation defense

学生在器件实验室做实验

Students in the device laboratory

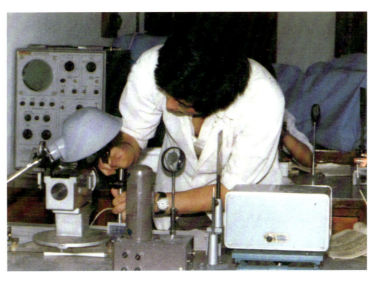

学生在实验室做实验

Students doing experiments

2. 国际交流 International Exchanges

1984年5月，副校长忻福良陪同联邦德国驻上海总领事参观上海科技专科学校电教演播室
Consul-General of Federal Germany in Shanghai, accompanied by Vice President Xin Fuliang, visiting the audio-visual studio of SCST, May 1984

1985年，校长钱孝衡（前排右一）与到访的美国艾奥瓦大学谭默教授（前排右二）合影（背景是学校老校门）
President Qian Xiaoheng (first from right in the front row) with the visiting professor (second from right in the front row) from the University of Iowa, 1985

1987年，英国西格拉摩根高等教育学院院长偕夫人到上海科技专科学校参观访问
President of West Glamorgan College of Higher Education visiting SCST, 1987

获全国荣誉称号人员
Faculty Winning National Honors

荣誉称号	年 度	姓名
全国优秀教师	1989	朱锡仁

钱伟长与徐匡迪(油画)
Qian Weichang and Xu Kuangdi (oil painting)

第三部分

1994年至今的上海大学

1994年4月25日，国家教育委员会批文同意上海市人民政府关于上海工业大学、上海科学技术大学、上海大学和上海科技高等专科学校合并建立上海大学的请示。

新时期的上海大学，是国家"211工程"重点建设的综合性大学、教育部与上海市人民政府共建高校、教育部"双一流"建设高校。上海大学正在努力建设成为世界一流特色鲜明的综合性研究型大学。

Part III

Shanghai University from 1994 to Now

On April 25, 1994, the National Education Commission approved the application of Shanghai Municipal People's Government for the merger of SUT, SUST, SHU, and SCST to establish a new SHU.

SHU in the new era is a comprehensive university jointly built by the Ministry of Education and Shanghai Municipal People's Government, amongst the list of "Project 211" and "Double First Class" for top national universities. SHU is now striving to be ranked as a world-leading research-intensive comprehensive university with distinctive features.

一

合并组建

Merger and Establishment

校训：自强不息；先天下之忧而忧，后天下之乐而乐

校风：求实创新

School Motto: Pursuing excellence; Being the first to share the world's woes and the last to rejoice in its weal

School Spirit: Seeking truth and innovations

（一）新上海大学成立
Establishment of New SHU

1994年5月27日，校长钱伟长与中共上海市委副书记、市长黄菊一起，为新上海大学揭牌

President Qian Weichang and Huang Ju, Mayor of Shanghai, unveiling the new SHU, May 27, 1994

1994年5月27日，新上海大学成立大会在上海展览中心友谊会堂举行

The founding conference of the new SHU in the Friendship Hall of Shanghai Exhibition Center, May 27, 1994

第三部分　1994年至今的上海大学　　　　　　　　　　　　　　　　　　　　　一、合并组建

1994年5月27日，校长钱伟长在新上海大学成立大会上讲话
President Qian Weichang delivering a speech at the founding conference of the new SHU, May 27, 1994

1994年5月27日，中共上海市委副书记陈至立、市教委主任郑令德与新上海大学领导班子合影。左起：巡视员李明忠、巡视员余忠荪、副校长沈学超、常务副校长杨德广、纪委书记廖由雄、党委副书记毛杏云、郑令德、副校长壮云乾、校长钱伟长、副校长龚振邦、陈至立、副校长陈大森、党委书记吴程里、巡视员汪国铎、党委副书记杨慧如、巡视员徐得名、常务副校长方明伦、副校长黄黔
Chen Zhili, Deputy Secretary of the CPC Shanghai Municipal Committee, and Zheng Lingde, Director of Shanghai Municipal Education Committee, and the leaders of the new SHU, May 27, 1994

183

上海大学

1994年5月4日，中共中央总书记、国家主席、中央军委主席江泽民为上海大学题写校名

The name of SHU calligraphed by Jiang Zemin, General Secretary of the CPC Central Committee, President of the PRC, and Chairman of the Central Military Commission, May 4, 1994

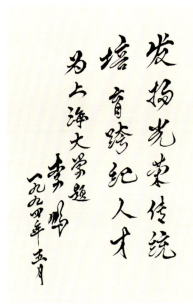

1994年5月，中共中央政治局常委、国务院总理李鹏为上海大学题词

An inscription for SHU by Li Peng, a member of the Standing Committee of the Political Bureau of the CPC Central Committee and Premier of the State Council, May 1994

1994年5月，原国家主席、老上海大学学生杨尚昆为上海大学题词

An inscription for SHU by Yang Shangkun, former President of the PRC and student of SHU (1922-1927), May 1994

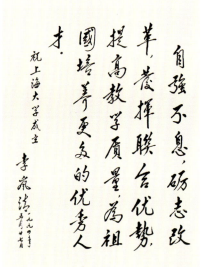

1994年5月27日，中共中央政治局委员、国务院副总理李岚清为上海大学题词

An inscription for SHU by Li Lanqing, a member of the Political Bureau of the CPC Central Committee and Vice Premier of the State Council, May 27, 1994

（二）新校区建设
Construction of the New Campus

1997年，中共上海市委书记黄菊、市委副书记龚学平审看新校区规划模型

Huang Ju, Secretary of the CPC Shanghai Municipal Committee, and Gong Xueping, Deputy Secretary of the CPC Shanghai Municipal Committee, reviewing the layout of the new campus, 1997

1999年9月12日，举行新校区启用暨开学典礼

The opening ceremony of the new campus, September 12, 1999

1999年11月，校长钱伟长陪同中共中央政治局常委、国务院副总理李岚清，教育部部长陈至立视察新校区

Vice Premier Li Lanqing, a member of the Standing Committee of the Political Bureau of the CPC Central Committee, and Chen Zhili, Minister of Education, inspecting the new campus, accompanied by President Qian Weichang, November 1999

二

改革与战略发展
Reform and Strategic Development

（一）各级领导关心学校发展
Visits of Leaders

2005年5月18日，全国政协副主席、中共中央统战部部长刘延东来校看望钱伟长校长

Liu Yandong, Vice Chairman of the National Committee of the CPPCC and Minister of the United Front Work Department of the CPC Central Committee, visiting President Qian Weichang, May 18, 2005

2005年9月11日，中共中央政治局常委、全国政协主席贾庆林来校看望钱伟长校长

Jia Qinglin, a member of the Standing Committee of the Political Bureau of the CPC Central Committee and Chairman of the National Committee of the CPPCC, visiting President Qian Weichang, September 11, 2005

2008年6月18日,中共中央政治局委员、上海市委书记俞正声,市委副书记殷一璀,市委办公厅主任丁薛祥来校调研和考察
Yu Zhengsheng, a member of the Political Bureau of the CPC Central Committee and Secretary of the CPC Shanghai Municipal Committee, Yin Yicui, Deputy Secretary of the CPC Shanghai Municipal Committee, and Ding Xuexiang, Director of the General Office of the CPC Shanghai Municipal Committee, visiting SHU, June 18, 2008

2014年6月16日,全国政协副主席、科技部部长万钢来校视察
Wan Gang, Vice Chairman of the National Committee of the CPPCC and Minister of Science and Technology, visiting SHU, June 16, 2014

第三部分　1994年至今的上海大学　　　　　二、改革与战略发展

2016年3月23日，中共中央政治局委员、上海市委书记韩正来校调研和考察
Han Zheng, a member of the Political Bureau of the CPC Central Committee and Secretary of the CPC Shanghai Municipal Committee, visiting SHU, March 23, 2016

2017年7月27日，中共上海市委副书记尹弘来校调研和考察
Yin Hong, Deputy Secretary of the CPC Shanghai Municipal Committee, inspecting the Party work of SHU, July 27, 2017

2019年12月30日，中共中央政治局委员、上海市委书记李强来校调研和考察

Li Qiang, a member of the Political Bureau of the CPC Central Committee and Secretary of the CPC Shanghai Municipal Committee, visiting SHU, December 30, 2019

2020年3月13日，中共上海市委副书记廖国勋来校调研和考察

Liao Guoxun, Deputy Secretary of the CPC Shanghai Municipal Committee, visiting SHU, March 13, 2020

（二）"211工程"建设
Implementation of the "Project 211" Construction

1996年12月23日，举行"211工程"部门预审开幕式

The opening ceremony of the pre-examination of the "Project 211," December 23, 1996

2002年3月19—20日，召开"211工程""九五"期间建设项目（一期）验收会

The acceptance meeting of the "Project 211" and the "Ninth Five-Year Plan" projects (Phase I), March 19-20, 2002

2006年6月17—18日,召开"211工程""十五"期间建设项目(二期)验收会
The acceptance meeting of the "Project 211" and the "Tenth Five-Year Plan" projects (Phase II), June 17-18, 2006

2012年3月18日,召开"211工程"建设项目(三期)验收会
The acceptance meeting of the "Project 211" (Phase III), March 18, 2012

（三）专业技术职务聘任制改革
Reform on the Promotion System

2001年11月，校党委书记、常务副校长方明伦主持教师专业技术职务聘任委员会会议

Fang Minglun, Secretary of the Party Committee and Executive Vice President of SHU, presiding over the meeting on the promotion system for the faculty, November 2001

2003年2月13日，召开实验室管理改革动员会，引入"技术总监"岗位聘任制（左起：副校长曹家麟，常务副校长周哲玮，校党委书记方明伦，校党委副书记、副校长周鸿刚）

The meeting on laboratory management reform, introducing Chief Technology Officer to the post track, February 13, 2003

（四）本科教学工作水平评估
Assessment of the Undergraduate Teaching Qualification

2003年10月20日，举行教育部普通高等学校本科教学工作水平评估上海大学校长汇报会

President of SHU reporting on the undergraduate teaching work during the assessment of the undergraduate teaching qualification carried out by the Ministry of Education, October 20, 2003

2004年6月16日，《教育部办公厅关于公布上海大学等42所高等学校本科教学工作评估结论的通知》（教高厅〔2004〕19号）公布上海大学等20所学校本科教学工作的评估结论为优秀

The Notice of granting SHU "Excellent" grade in undergraduate teaching, by the General Office of the Ministry of Education, June 16, 2004

（五）确立钱伟长教育思想
Establishment of Qian Weichang's Educational Thought

2007年1月12日，校党委书记于信汇在代表校领导班子作的报告中，明确提出"钱伟长教育思想"

Yu Xinhui, Secretary of the Party Committee of SHU, proposing to establish Qian Weichang's educational thought, January 12, 2007

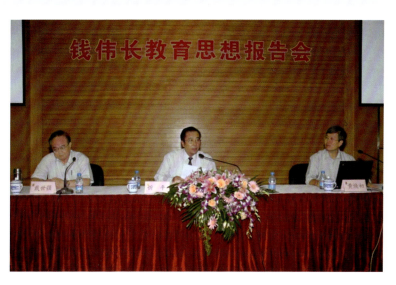

2007年10月9日，校党委副书记忻平主持钱伟长教育思想报告会

Xin Ping, Deputy Secretary of the Party Committee, presiding over the seminar on Qian Weichang's educational thought, October 9, 2007

2020年7月30日，举行"钱伟长星"命名仪式暨钱伟长画传首发式。图为"钱伟长教育思想与上海大学改革发展"主题座谈会会场，正面一排左起：戴世强、曾文彪、叶志明、刘宇陆、成旦红、刘晓明、欧阳华、翁培奋、傅克诚

The naming ceremony of "Qian Weichang Planet" and book release of *President Qian Weichang: A Photobiography*, July 30, 2020. A seminar on Qian Weichang's Educational Thought and Reform & Development of SHU was held later that day.

（六）召开战略发展专家咨询会
Forum on the Development Strategy of SHU

2004年5月6日，召开"上海大学战略发展专家咨询会"，副校长周哲玮主持会议，校党委书记、常务副校长方明伦致辞并介绍学校情况，中国工程院副院长王淀佐院士作"屹立于我国和世界名校之林"的讲话，海内外20多所大学的领导出席会议

The forum on the development strategy of SHU, attended by leaders from more than 20 international universities, May 6, 2004

（七）成为国家建设高水平大学公派研究生项目签约院校
A New Member in China Scholarship Council Postgraduate Scholarship Program

2009年10月12日，上海大学成为国家建设高水平大学公派研究生项目签约院校

SHU participating in the signing ceremony of Postgraduate Study Abroad Program for High-Level University Construction funded by China Scholarship Council, October 12, 2009

（八）成立董事会
Establishment of SHU Board of Trustees

2012年5月27日，举行校董事会成立大会暨首届校董会第一次会议，校党委书记于信汇、校长罗宏杰出席会议，第十届全国政协副主席、中国工程院原院长、中国工程院主席团名誉主席徐匡迪院士担任首届校董事会主席
The inaugural meeting of the SHU Board of Trustees, Academician Xu Kuangdi serving as the first Board Chairman, May 27, 2012

2017年5月27日，举行第二届校董事会第一次会议，校党委书记罗宏杰、校长金东寒出席会议，中国工程院院士、原副院长、中国金属学会理事长干勇担任董事会主席
The first meeting of the second SHU Board of Trustees, Academician Gan Yong serving as the second Board Chairman, May 27, 2017

2019年9月21日，举行第二届校董事会第三次会议，校党委书记成旦红、校长刘昌胜出席会议

The third meeting of the second SHU Board of Trustees, attended by Secretary of the Party Committee of SHU Cheng Danhong and President Liu Changsheng, September 21, 2019

（九）成为教育部与上海市共建高校　Co-construction of SHU by the Ministry of Education and Shanghai Municipal People's Government

2013年4月18日，教育部、上海市人民政府共建上海大学协议签字仪式在北京举行，教育部部长、党组书记袁贵仁，上海市市长杨雄出席签约仪式；上海市副市长翁铁慧与教育部副部长鲁昕签署《关于共建上海大学的协议》

The signing ceremony of the agreement between the Ministry of Education and Shanghai Municipal People's Government on jointly building SHU, April 18, 2013

（十）建设环上大产业园、科技园区
Construction of SHU Rim Industrial Park and Science and Technology Park

2014年11月26日，中共中央政治局委员、上海市委书记韩正视察环上大影视产业园区
Han Zheng, a member of the Political Bureau of the CPC Central Committee and Secretary of the CPC Shanghai Municipal Committee, inspecting the SHU Rim Industrial Park on Film and Television, November 26, 2014

2015年6月5日，由中国社会科学院与上海市人民政府共同创建的新型智库上海研究院在延长校区成立
The univeiling ceremony of Shanghai Academy, a new-type think tank co-founded by the Chinese Academy of Social Sciences and Shanghai Municipal People's Government, June 5, 2015

2020年6月22日，环上大科技园揭牌，学校与宝山区携手打造示范性创新创业集聚区
The unveiling ceremony of SHU Rim Science and Technology Park, June 22, 2020

党的建设
Party Building

（一）加强党的建设和校领导班子建设
Improvement of Party Building and Leadership Construction

1995年1月18日，召开第一次党的建设工作会议，首次提出"围绕中心抓党建、抓好党建促中心、检验党建看中心"的党建工作理念。1998年后在向全市推广时，市教卫工作党委改为"检验党建看发展"
The first Party building conference of SHU, January 18, 1995

1999年，校领导集体合影（前排左起：党委副书记、副校长周鸿刚，党委副书记毛杏云，校长钱伟长，党委书记、常务副校长方明伦，党委副书记杨慧如；后排左起：校长助理刘晓明，副校长周哲玮，副校长王奇，副校长沈学超，副校长壮云乾，巡视员刘德重，副校长龚振邦，副校长夏玲英）
Group photo of SHU leaders, 1999

百年上大 画传

2004年5月，校领导集体合影（前排左起：副校长叶志明，副校长曹家麟，党委副书记沈学超，党委书记、常务副校长方明伦，校长钱伟长，党委副书记、副校长周鸿刚，副校长周哲玮，副校长李友梅，副校长金国华；后排左起：校秘书长曾文彪，校长助理汪敏，巡视员薛志良，工会主席壮云乾，巡视员唐豪，校长助理刘宇陆，校长助理俞涛，总经济师张平伟）

Group photo of SHU leaders, May 2004

2007年1月12日，召开中国共产党上海大学第一次代表大会。图为第一届党委委员合影

Group photo of the members of the First CPC Committee of SHU after the First CPC Congress of SHU, January 13, 2007

202

第三部分　1994年至今的上海大学　　　　　　　　　　　　　　　　　　　　　　　　　三、党的建设

2013年6月26日，召开中国共产党上海大学第二次代表大会。图为大会会场
The Second CPC Congress of SHU, June 26, 2013

2018年6月29日，召开中国共产党上海大学第三次代表大会。图为第三届委员会全体委员合影
Group photo of the members of the Third CPC Committee of SHU after the Third CPC Congress of SHU, June 30, 2018

党建工作荣誉
Honors in Party Building

党的建设和思想政治工作先进普通高等学校		
荣誉名称	获奖单位	文件名称
1993—1998 党的建设和思想政治工作先进普通高等学校	上海大学	中组部、中宣部、教育部党组关于表彰 1993—1998 党的建设和思想政治工作先进普通高等学校的决定，教党〔1998〕14 号

首批全国党建工作示范单位		
荣誉名称	获奖单位	文件名称
首批"全国党建工作标杆院系"培育创建单位	上海大学理学院党委	教育部办公厅关于公布首批全国党建工作示范高校、标杆院系、样板支部培育创建单位名单的通知，教思政厅函〔2018〕43 号
首批"全国党建工作样板支部"培育创建单位	上海大学通信与信息工程学院特种光纤与光接入网党支部	
首批高校"百个研究生样板党支部"创建单位	上海大学社会科学学部 2016 级硕士研究生党支部	教育部办公厅关于公布首批高校"百个研究生样板党支部""百名研究生党员标兵"创建名单的通知，教思政厅函〔2019〕2 号

（二）党建主题教育
Theme Education on Party Building

2005年11月14日，召开党员先进性教育活动总结大会
The summary conference of the Educational Campaign to Preserve the Vanguard Nature of CPC Members, November 14, 2005

2008年10月20日，召开开展深入学习实践科学发展观活动动员大会
The mobilization meeting for Implementation of the Scientific Outlook on Development, October 20, 2008

2019年9月10日，召开"不忘初心、牢记使命"主题教育动员部署会
The mobilization and deployment meeting for "Remaining True to Our Mission" Campaign, September 10, 2019

百年上大 画传

2019年11月15日，召开新时代、新青年、新使命——"我与校长面对面"主题座谈会
A Face-to-Face Talk with Presidents, featuring New Youth and New Mission in the New Era, November 15, 2019

2020年3月24日，召开第二十四次党的建设工作会议暨2020年全面从严治党工作会议
The 24th Party Building Conference of SHU, March 24, 2020

教育教学改革

Educational Reform

（一）适应学科建设需要，成立新的学院
Establishment of New Colleges to Meet the Needs of Discipline Construction

1994年9月，成立知识产权学院。图为知识产权学院学生参加模拟法庭时的合影

Students of the Intellectual Property College, established in September 1994, taking part in a mock court trial

1995年5月19日，召开影视艺术技术学院、生命科学学院、外国语学院成立大会（左起：生命科学学院院长杨雄里院士、中共上海市委副秘书长周慕尧、校长钱伟长、上海市副市长龚学平、影视艺术技术学院院长谢晋、常务副校长方明伦、常务副校长杨德广）

The founding conference of the School of Film and Television Arts and Technology, the School of Life Sciences, and the School of Foreign Languages, May 19, 1995

2013年6月2日，成立音乐学院，第十届全国政协副主席、中国工程院原院长、中国工程院主席团名誉主席徐匡迪，全国人大常委会委员、教育部原副部长吴启迪共同为音乐学院揭牌

The founding ceremony of the Music School, June 2, 2013

2014年6月15日，成立上海温哥华电影学院。图为2016年9月5日贾樟柯院长上开学第一课

Jia Zhangke, a famous Chinese director, serving as Dean of Shanghai Vancouver Film School, founded on June 15, 2014

2015年7月5日，成立上海大学上海电影学院，中共上海市教卫工作党委书记陈克宏（右二）、上海市文化广播影视管理局局长胡劲军（右一）与罗宏杰校长、陈凯歌院长（左二）共同为上海大学上海电影学院揭牌

The unveiling ceremony of SHU Shanghai Film Academy, July 5, 2015

2016年12月11日，成立上海大学上海美术学院，上海市副市长翁铁慧（左）与院长冯远共同开启"上海美术学院之门"

The founding ceremony of Shanghai Academy of Fine Arts of SHU, December 11, 2016

2017年7月6日，举行文教结合共建上海美术学院签约暨上海吴淞国际艺术城发展研究院揭牌仪式，上海市副市长翁铁慧、校长金东寒等出席

The signing ceremony on the joint construction of Shanghai Academy of Fine Arts and the opening ceremony of the Development Research Institute of Shanghai Wusong International Art City, July 6, 2017

2018年10月20日，成立新闻传播学院，中共上海市委宣传部副部长朱咏雷（右）与校党委书记、校长金东寒共同为新闻传播学院揭牌

The founding ceremony of the School of Journalism and Communication, October 20, 2018

2019年9月8日，成立力学与工程科学学院，校长刘昌胜院士（左二）、杨卫院士（右二）、方岱宁院士（左一）和郭兴明教授（右一）共同为力学与工程科学学院揭牌

The founding ceremony of the School of Mechanics and Engineering Science, September 8, 2019

2020年6月6日，成立医工交叉研究院，上海市副市长陈群、市政府副秘书长虞丽娟、市教卫工作党委书记沈炜等共同为医工交叉研究院揭牌

The founding ceremony of the SHU Medical-Engineering Cross Research Institute, June 6, 2020

（二）加强本科教学、招生改革工作
Deepening Reform on Undergraduate Teaching and Enrollment System

2003 年 10 月，校长钱伟长出席教育部上海大学本科教学工作水平评估专家意见反馈会并讲话

President Qian Weichang delivering a speech at the feedback meeting of the undergraduate teaching qualification assessment by the Ministry of Education, October 2003

2009 年，教育部正式批准上海大学进行自主招生选拔录取改革试点。从 2011 年起，学校全面推行以大类招生和通识教育培养为突破口的本科教育教学改革

In 2009, the Ministry of Education officially approved SHU to carry out the pilot reform of independent enrollment. Since 2011, SHU has been carrying out the reform on undergraduate education and teaching with general education as the breakthrough point.

2018 年 5 月 26 日，副校长聂清（左一）参加 2018 年招生信息发布会暨本科招生咨询会

Vice President Nie Qing attending the 2018 enrollment information announcement meeting and undergraduate enrollment consultation meeting, May 26, 2018

（三）重视研究生教育
Cultivation of Graduate Students

2013年10月25日，校党委书记于信汇、校长罗宏杰、副校长叶志明、副校长吴明红等出席上海大学研究生院成立大会

Secretary of the Party Committee of SHU Yu Xinhui, President Luo Hongjie, Vice President Ye Zhiming and Vice President Wu Minghong attending the inaugural meeting of the Graduate School of SHU, October 25, 2013

2019年4月1日，全国政协委员、副校长汪小帆为研究生作"从'两会'看当代研究生的使命担当"专题讲座

Wang Xiaofan, a member of the National Committee of the CPPCC and Vice President of SHU, giving a lecture on "The Mission and Responsibility of Contemporary Graduate Students," April 1, 2019

2019年9月1日，举行2019级研究生开学典礼暨入学教育

The opening ceremony of the 2019 new intake graduate students, September 1, 2019

（四）思政教学创新
Innovations in Ideological and Political Teaching

2011年4月21日，教育部副部长李卫红等到"毛泽东思想和中国特色社会主义理论体系概论"课堂听课（主讲胡申生、顾晓英）

Li Weihong, Vice Minister of Education, attending a course on Mao Zedong Thought and the theory of socialism with Chinese characteristics lectured by Hu Shensheng and Gu Xiaoying, April 21, 2011

2014年12月11日，中宣部副部长王世明（左三）等来校调研，到"大国方略"课堂听课（主讲李梁、顾晓英）

Wang Shiming (third from left), Vice Minister of the Publicity Department of the CPC Central Committee, inspecting the course "What Matters to Rising China?" lectured by Li Liang and Gu Xiaoying, December 11, 2014

2014年12月17日，中央电视台报道上海大学"大国方略"课程

CCTV reporting on the course "What Matters to Rising China?" of SHU, December 17, 2014

2015年10月，"大国方略"教学团队获中央宣传部办公厅授予的"基层理论宣讲先进集体"称号

The teaching team of "What Matters to Rising China?" awarded "Outstanding Unit of Theory Teaching" by the General Office of the Publicity Department of the CPC Central Committee, October 2015

第三部分　1994年至今的上海大学　　　　四、教育教学改革

2015年3月31日，"大国方略"课程团队进行教学研讨
Team members of the course "What Matters to Rising China?" conducting a teaching seminar, March 31, 2015

2018年3月26日，举行育才大工科——"人工智能"公开课（主讲顾骏、郭毅可）
An open class of the general education course "Artificial Intelligence" lectured by Gu Jun and Guo Yike, March 26, 2018

2018年1月16日，校党委书记、校长金东寒在全国"加强新时代高校思政理论课建设现场推进会"上作经验交流
Jin Donghan, Secretary of the Party Committee and President of SHU, sharing the experience of SHU at the National Conference on Strengthening the Construction of Ideological and Political Courses in the New Era, January 16, 2018

2019年6月28日，校党委书记成旦红为2019届本科毕业生上思想政治课
Cheng Danhong, Secretary of the Party Committee of SHU, giving a lecture on ideology and politics for the Class of 2019, June 28, 2019

（五）国家级精品课程、教学团队和教学成果奖
National Quality Courses, Teaching Teams, and Teaching Achievements

国家级精品课程
National Quality Courses

课程名称	课程负责人	获批年度	类　别
土木工程概论	叶志明	2005	国家级精品课
档案学导论	金　波	2009	国家级精品课
工程力学	陈立群	2010	国家级精品课
商标纠纷矛与盾	陶鑫良	2014	国家精品视频公开课
品味物理	姜　颖	2014	国家精品视频公开课
成为作家	葛红兵	2015	国家精品视频公开课
创新中国	顾　骏 顾晓英	2017	国家精品在线开放课程
土木工程概论	叶志明	2018	国家精品在线开放课程

国家级教学团队
National Teaching Teams

团队名称	负责人	获批年度
土木工程专业学科基础课程教学团队	叶志明	2008
社会学基础课程教学团队	李友梅	2009

国家级教学成果奖及部分获奖证书
National Teaching Achievements and Some Certificates

成果名称	主要完成人	级　别	获奖年度	主要完成单位
入耳入脑入心　同向同行同频：以思政课为核心的课程思政教育教学改革与创新	许宁生　焦　扬　陈锡喜 沙　军　赵宪忠　褚君浩 姜智彬　刘淑慧　顾铮先 曹文泽　李　梁　张黎声 李　江　李国娟　吴　强 桂永浩　顾钰民　宗爱东	一等奖	2018	复旦大学、上海交通大学、上海市教育科学研究院、同济大学、华东师范大学、上海外国语大学、东华大学、上海理工大学、华东政法大学、上海大学、上海中医药大学、上海工程技术大学、上海应用技术大学、上海政法学院
土木工程类课程教学改革的研究与实践	叶志明　汪德江　徐　旭 宋少沪　张　凌	二等奖	2001	上海大学
问题导向的思想政治理论课"项链模式"改革与创新	忻　平　王天恩　李　梁 顾晓英　魏　宏　张丹华 林自强　谢宝婷　申小翠 奚建群	二等奖	2014	上海大学
构建基于大数据分析的常态化教育教学质量监控与保障体系	叶志明　宋少沪　辛明军 王光东　陈方泉　叶　红 郭长刚　田蔚文　楚丹琪 于海阳	二等奖	2014	上海大学
对照国际标准，强化工艺能力，培养高水平数控技术人才的创新与实践	鞠鲁粤　张　萍　陆建刚 刘　霞　林成辉　李　斌 姜锡鲁　傅丰伟　陈　觉 刘　涛	二等奖	2014	上海大学
"大国方略"系列课程的创设与实践	顾晓英　顾　骏　聂永有 刘寅斌　肖俊杰　罗　均 张新鹏　忻　平　李友梅 狄其安　叶志明　王海松 王国中　许　斌　许春明	二等奖	2018	上海大学

2001年12月,"土木工程类课程教学改革的研究与实践"获国家级教学成果奖二等奖
"Research and Practice of Civil Engineering Course Reform" winning the Second Prize of National Teaching Achievement Award, December 2001

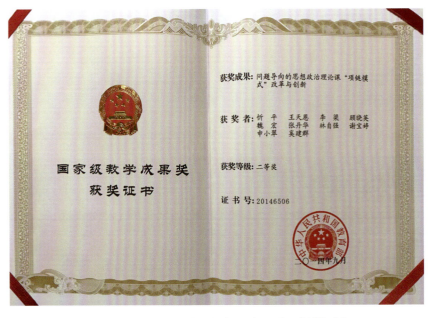

2014年9月,"问题导向的思想政治理论课'项链模式'改革与创新"获国家级教学成果奖二等奖
"Reform and Innovation of the 'Necklace Mode' of Problem-Oriented Ideological and Political Theory Courses" winning the Second Prize of National Teaching Achievement Award, September 2014

2018年12月,"'大国方略'系列课程的创设与实践"获国家级教学成果奖二等奖
The "What Matters to Rising China?" course series winning the Second Prize of National Teaching Achievement Award, December 2018

全国普通高等学校优秀教材及部分获奖证书
National Excellent Textbooks Award and Some Certificates

教材名称	编著者姓名	级别	获奖年度	编著者单位
国际贸易理论与实务	陈宪　韦金鸾　应诚敏　陈晨	二等奖	2002	上海大学
液压与气压传动	章宏甲　黄谊　王积伟	二等奖	2002	东南大学　上海大学
土木工程概论CAI	叶志明　汪德江　宋少沪　徐旭	二等奖	2002	上海大学
传播学通论	戴元光　金冠军	二等奖	2002	上海大学

2002年10月，叶志明教授等编著的《土木工程概论CAI》获全国普通高等学校优秀教材二等奖
Computer Aided Instruction for the Introduction to Civil Engineering, co-edited by Professor Ye Zhiming et al., winning the Second Prize of National Excellent Textbooks Award, October 2002

2002年10月，影视艺术技术学院教师戴元光、金冠军编著的《传播学通论》获全国普通高等学校优秀教材二等奖
Theories of Communication, co-edited by Dai Yuanguang and Jin Guanjun, teachers of the School of Film and Television Arts and Technology, winning the Second Prize of National Excellent Textbooks Award, October 2002

五

人才培养
Talent Cultivation

（一）成立社区学院、钱伟长学院
Establishment of Residential College and QianWeiChang College

践行钱伟长"培养学生更重要的在课外"的思想，建立课外培养平台，成立社区学院。2007年11月28日，常务副校长周哲玮为社区学院揭牌

Vice President Zhou Zhewei, unveiling the Residential College, established as an extracurricular training platform following Qian Weichang's thought that "Extracurricular activities are more important to student cultivation," November 28, 2007

2011年，自强学院获批国家试点学院并更名为钱伟长学院，10月9日上海市教卫工作党委书记李宣海（右）、校党委书记于信汇共同为钱伟长学院揭牌

The unveiling ceremony of the QianWeiChang College, attended by Li Xuanhai (right), Secretary of the CPC Committee of Shanghai Municipal Education and Health Work, and Yu Xinhui, Secretary of the Party Committee of SHU, October 9, 2011

（二）设立奖学金
Setup of Scholarships

1994年10月17日，举行"光华奖学金"颁奖大会，校党委书记吴程里（中）、常务副校长杨德广（左三）、常务副校长郭本瑜（左四）等出席

The Guanghua Scholarship Award Ceremony, October 17, 1994

2006年3月30日，校长钱伟长与首届"校长奖学金"获奖学生亲切交谈

President Qian Weichang talking with the first President Scholarship winners, March 30, 2006

2009年2月，举行费孝通教育奖学金颁奖典礼
The Fei Xiaotong Education Scholarship Award Ceremony, February 2009

2011年，举行2009—2010学年蔡冠深奖学金颁奖典礼
The Choi Koon Shum Scholarship Award Ceremony, 2011

2013年5月3日，举行2012年度研究生国家奖学金颁奖典礼
The 2012 National Postgraduate Scholarship Award Ceremony, May 3, 2013

（三）助力成才、支持创新创业
Supports on Talent Cultivation and Innovative Enterpreneurship

2005年12月19日，校长钱伟长以导师身份出席上海市应用数学和力学研究所周文波（后排右二）博士论文答辩会。周文波是钱伟长在1990年招收的硕士研究生，入学前是一位仅有职工业余大学学历的工人

President Qian Weichang attending the doctoral dissertation defense of Zhou Wenbo (second from right in the back row) of Shanghai Institute of Applied Mathematics and Mechanics as his supervisor, December 19, 2005. Zhou, who used to be a worker with a part-time university degree, was recruited by Qian Weichang as a graduate student in 1990.

2007年2月11日，校党委副书记滕建勇走访困难学生

Teng Jianyong, Deputy Secretary of the Party Committee of SHU, visiting a needy student, February 11, 2007

2007年4月13日，人才学院师生结对
The pairing ceremony of teachers and students of the Talent Institute, April 13, 2007

生命科学学院2011级生物工程本科生付思艺作为第一作者在国际期刊《细胞与分子医学杂志》上发表题为《人肝纤维化中的特洛细胞》的论文
Fu Siyi, an undergraduate of biological engineering of the School of Life Sciences, the first author of "Telocytes in Human Liver Fibrosis" in *Journal of Cellular and Molecular Medicine*

社会学院本科生阿里木江·于山获2013年度"中国大学生自强之星"
Alimujiang Yushan, an undergraduate of the School of Sociology and Political Science, awarded the title of the 2013 "Self-improvement Star of Chinese College Students"

2017年6月23日，校党委副书记徐旭出席上海大学紫荆谷创新创业辅导中心成立暨上海大学创新创业学院——紫荆谷·跨境通战略合作启动仪式

The launching ceremony of SHU-Bauhinia Valley Innovation and Enterpreneurship Counseling Center, attended by Xu Xu, Deputy Secretary of the Party Committee of SHU, June 23, 2017

2019年1月4日，举行2018年度本科生学术论坛颁奖典礼，孙晋良院士、副校长聂清出席

The award ceremony of the 2018 SHU Academic Forum for Undergraduates, January 4, 2019

2019年1月21日，举行高水平大学拔尖创新人才培养项目申报答辩、评审会，副校长汪小帆出席

The defense and evaluation meeting of top-level innovative talent training programs, chaired by Vice President Wang Xiaofan, January 21, 2019

（四）参加全国及国际竞赛，培养创新能力
Awards in National and International Competitions

2017年11月18日，在第十五届"挑战杯"竞赛总决赛中获团体第二，捧得"优胜杯"
SHU won the "Winning Cup" in the 15th "Challenge Cup," a national competition known as the "Olympics" of science and technology for Chinese college students, November 18, 2017.

历届"挑战杯"全国大学生课外学术科技作品竞赛获奖
Awards in the "Challenge Cup"

序号	获奖学院	作品名称	学生负责人	团队成员	指导老师	奖项	年度	届别
1	材料学院	塑料模具钢表面抛光性能光学评定系统及应用	谢尘		汪宏斌	一等奖	2009	第十一届
2	悉尼工商学院	轨道交通车站施工安全监测与软件分析	包怡龄	包怡龄 赵莉 林璐璐	胡珉	一等奖	2011	第十二届
3	社会学院	上海市蒙维藏少数民族大学生族群认同研究	张广楚	张广楚 胡安琪 巴依尔 史心怡 姜晟	耿敬 张江华	一等奖	2011	第十二届
4	理学院	基于柱[5]芳烃和双咪唑盐的准轮烷型分子开关	赵浏		李春举	一等奖	2011	第十二届

（续表）

序号	获奖学院	作品名称	学生负责人	团队成员	指导老师	奖项	年度	届别
5	理学院	水溶性柱[5]芳烃对碱性氨基酸的选择性键合研究	马俊伟		李春举	一等奖	2013	第十三届
6	社会学院	流浪儿童何以"流浪"——对新疆流浪儿童成因与对策研究	阿里木江·于山	周雨薇 章世园 帕提哈西·塔拉甫别克 夏兆强 曹诗婕	耿敬	特等奖	2013	第十三届
7	美术学院	让非遗"活"在当下——黔东南地区苗绣艺人生活现况的调查研究	杨子爱（研）	刘璐（研） 闫利（研） 高欣	陈青	一等奖	2015	第十四届
8	社会学院	从人生炼狱到圆梦天堂——以亚洲最大高考工厂毛坦厂中学为例	孙睿	程子杰 闵兰 徐玲枫 张梦笛	张江华	一等奖	2015	第十四届
9	材料科学与工程学院	一组适用于绿色建筑的智能调温调湿材料	窦维维	张志华 李小雨 方雅思 宋炳坷	高彦峰	一等奖	2017	第十五届
10	通信与信息工程学院	多维视觉卒中后手功能康复定量评估平台	赵泽伟	王聪 陆雅婷 王桥元 张天	陆小锋	特等奖	2017	第十五届
11	生命科学学院	基于抗结直肠癌活性SGK1抑制剂的结构修饰、合成与活性研究	梁绪春	兰春岭 付文成 安玉 焦冠铭	肖俊杰	特等奖	2017	第十五届
12	文学院	百年风华，劳工神圣——有关"一战"华工文化记忆的调查研究	徐嘉	郭艺颖 高昕 张若朴 刘胤衡 梅其右 杨智翔 邹涵璐	杨位俭	特等奖	2019	第十六届
13	管理学院	基于供应链金融的"三维信用评价体系"助力中小微企业融资增信——对140家企业和40家金融机构的访谈调研	谢天豪（研）	钱赛楠（研）张尊力（研）闫娅男（研）李欣怡（研）杨佩芳（研）艾浩然（研）谢冰（研）	储雪俭	特等奖	2019	第十六届
14	社会学院	公共服务资源供给与社区组织网络构建：以农村睦邻点为例的调查分析	蔡旻雯	文薇薇 丁志文 严俨 陈芳 刘畅 马晓宇	金桥	一等奖	2019	第十六届

2017年5月21日，上海大学自强队在2017中国服务机器人大赛仿真组赛上获得冠军

SHU students winning the championship in the simulation group of the 2017 China Service Robot Competition, May 21, 2017

2017年7月21日，Dream House团队在第三届全球重大挑战论坛"学生日"活动（竞赛）中位列中国高校第一，获得全球第三名

The Dream House team of SHU ranking the first among Chinese universities and the third among international universities in the Third Global Major Challenge Forum "Student Day," July 21, 2017

2017年8月22日，在第十二届中国研究生电子设计竞赛全国总决赛中获一等奖3个、二等奖2个及优秀组织奖

SHU students won 3 first prizes and 2 second prizes in the national final of the 12th China Graduate Student Electronic Design Competition, August 22, 2017. SHU won the Excellent Organization Prize.

（五）体育文艺人才辈出
Achievements in Sports and Cultural Activities

1994年上海大学男排被教育部命名为全国高校高水平运动队，代表上海市大学生分别在2000年、2004年、2008年获全国大学生运动会冠军，以上海大学学生为主的上海男排在1999—2019年间共获15次全国排球联赛冠军、2次全国运动会冠军

In 1994, the SHU Men's Volleyball Team was ranked the High-Level Sports Team by the Ministry of Education. It won 3 champions in the 2000, 2004, and 2008 National University Games as a representative of universities in Shanghai, and won 15 champions in National Volleyball Matches and 2 in National Games as main part in Shanghai Men's Volleyball Team from 1999 to 2019.

2008年9月，2005级学生王任杰参加北京残疾人奥运会获4×100米混合泳接力银牌

SHU student Wang Renjie, the silver medalist in the 4×100 meters medley relay at the Beijing Paralympics, September 2008

2009年12月，校网球运动员参加泛印度洋亚洲大学生运动会获网球女子团体冠军

The SHU tennis team, the winner of the women's tennis championship in the Pan-Indian Ocean Asian Universiade, December 2009

2011年8月，校网球运动员参加第二十六届世界大学生夏季运动会获网球项目双打亚军

The SHU tennis team, the winner of the Second Prize in tennis doubles in the 26th Summer Universiade, August 2011

2013年7月，留学生科菲在何颖强教练指导下参加世界大学生运动会，获100米第三名；2014年8月，获非洲田径锦标赛100米冠军；2015年5月，获国际田联挑战赛川崎站100米冠军

Koffi Hua Wilfried, an overseas student of SHU, winning the Third Prize in 100-meter race in the World University Games, July 2013, the First Prize in 100-meter race in the African Athletics Championships, August 2014, and the First Prize in 100-meter race in Kawasaki Station of IAAF Challenge Race, May 2015

2017年7月，校网球运动员参加第二十二届中国大学生网球锦标赛获女子丁组冠军

The SHU tennis team, the gold medalist of women's Group D in the 22nd China University Tennis Championships, July 2017

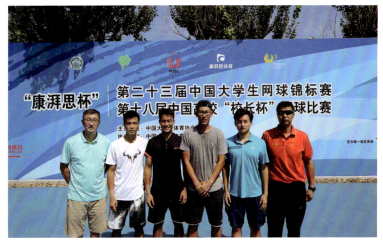

2018年8月，校网球运动员参加第二十三届中国大学生网球锦标赛获男子丁组团体冠军

The SHU tennis team, the gold medalist of men's Group D in the 23rd China University Tennis Championships, August 2018

2019年5月,校田径运动员宋佳媛参加亚洲田径锦标赛获女子铅球冠军

Song Jiayuan, champion of the women's shot in the Asian Athletics Championships, May 2019

2019年5月,校羽毛球运动员参加第七届中国大学生阳光体育羽毛球比赛获女双亚军

The SHU badminton team, the Second Prize winner of women's doubles in the seventh Sunny Sports Badminton Competition of National College Students, May 2019

2019年7月,校桥牌队参加中国大学生桥牌锦标赛获公开组乙级冠军

The SHU bridge team, the winner of the open Group B championship in the Chinese University Bridge Championships, July 2019

2005年7月，获全国第一届大学生艺术展演活动声乐节目普通组一等奖

The vocal music program winning the First Prize of the Non-professional Group in the First National Art Performances for College Students, July 2005

2009年2月，获全国第二届大学生艺术展演活动器乐节目甲组一等奖

SHU winning the First Prize of Instrumental Music Program Group A of the Second National Art Performances for College Students, February 2009

2015年3月，获全国第四届大学生艺术展演艺术表演类乙组一等奖

The SHU string orchestra winning the First Prize of Group B of the Fourth National Art Performances for College Students, March 2015

2018年4月，获全国第五届大学生艺术展演活动艺术表演类一等奖

The SHU choir winning the First Prize in the Fifth National Art Performances for College Students, April 2018

（六）毕业典礼，校长寄语
Graduation Ceremonies and Presidents' Addresses

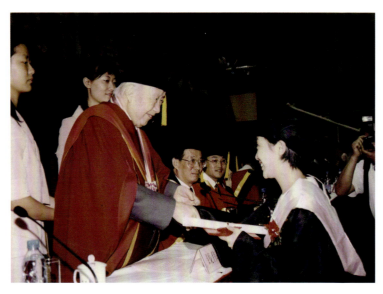

1995年6月，校长钱伟长向毕业生颁发学历证书
President Qian Weichang presenting diplomas to graduates, June 1995

2003年7月1日，常务副校长方明伦出席2003届优秀毕业生颁奖仪式暨毕业典礼
Executive Vice President Fang Minglun attending the graduation ceremony, July 1, 2003

2007年6月26日，常务副校长周哲玮出席研究生毕业典礼
Executive Vice President Zhou Zhewei attending the graduation ceremony for graduate students, June 26, 2007

2012年6月，校长罗宏杰出席2012届学生毕业典礼
President Luo Hongjie attending the graduation ceremony, June 2012

2016年6月25日，校长金东寒寄语2016届本科毕业生
President Jin Donghan addressing the graduates, June 25, 2016

2020年7月3日，校长刘昌胜寄语2020届本科毕业生
President Liu Changsheng addressing the graduates, July 3, 2020

毕业季

The graduation season

教育部授牌

Titles granted by the Ministry of Education

六

科学研究
Scientific Research

（一）重点实验室
Key Laboratories

省部共建高品质特殊钢冶金与制备国家重点实验室 先进钢铁材料技术国家工程研究中心南方实验基地
State Key Laboratory of Advanced Special Steel, also South Experimental Base of National Engineering and Research Center for Advanced Steel Technology

2015年5月4日，举行"省部共建高品质特殊钢冶金与制备国家重点实验室"揭牌仪式
The unveiling ceremony of the State Key Laboratory of Advanced Special Steel (SHU), May 4, 2015

特种光纤与光接入网省部共建教育部重点实验室
Key Laboratory of Specialty Fiber Optics and Optical Access Networks

新型显示技术及应用集成教育部重点实验室
TFTLCD关键材料及技术国家工程实验室
Key Laboratory of Advanced Display and System Applications, Ministry of Education, also State Engineering Laboratory for TFTLCD Key Materials and Technologies

材料复合与先进分散技术教育部工程研究中心
Engineering Research Center of Material Composition and Advanced Dispersion Technology, Ministry of Education

海洋智能无人系统装备教育部工程研究中心
Engineering Research Center of Marine Intelligent Unmanned Systems and Equipment, Ministry of Education

有机复合污染控制工程教育部重点实验室
Key Laboratory of Organic Compound Pollution Control Engineering, Ministry of Education

纳米复合功能材料国际科技合作示范基地
International Science and Technology Cooperation Base for Nanocomposite Functional Materials

（二）重要研究基地
Key Research Centers

1999年11月10日，上海社会发展研究中心成立。图为2001年9月校长钱伟长、上海社会发展研究中心主任费孝通教授与中心的教师座谈

President Qian Weichang and Professor Fei Xiaotong, Chair of the SHU Research Center of Social Development (established on November 10, 1999), talking with the members of the center, September 2001

2003年7月，科技园通过国家科技部和教育部验收，认定为国家级大学科技园

The Science and Technology Park of SHU was approved by the Ministry of Science and Technology and the Ministry of Education as a national university science and technology park in July 2003.

2008年3月31日，金属材料工程专业成为首个由教育部批准的国家级特色专业建设点的学科

Metal Material Engineering, the first discipline approved by the Ministry of Education as a national specialty program, March 31, 2008

2013年3月24日，校长罗宏杰与土耳其文化旅游部部长厄马尔·切利克共同出席上海大学土耳其研究中心揭牌仪式；2017年，土耳其研究中心成为学校首个由教育部批准备案建设的国别和区域研究中心

The unveiling ceremony of the Center for Turkish Studies at SHU, attended by President Luo Hongjie and Urmar Celik, Minister of Culture and Tourism, Turkey, March 24, 2013

2013年5月，举行国家体育总局与上海大学共建的"中国学校体育运动科学研究中心"揭牌暨共建签约仪式

The unveiling ceremony of the Research Center of Sport Science jointly built by SHU and the General Administration of Sport of China, May 2013

2015年11月2日，成立上海大学亚洲人口研究中心

The inauguration of the Institute for Asian Demographic Research of SHU, November 2, 2015

2017年4月12日，国家文物局局长刘玉珠、上海市副市长翁铁慧签署战略合作协议，10月19日，举行国家文物局与上海市人民政府共建的上海大学文化遗产保护基础科学研究院揭牌仪式暨丝绸之路文物科技创新联盟成立大会，上海市人大常委会副主任钟燕群、国家文物局副局长关强等出席

Liu Yuzhu, Director of the National Cultural Heritage Administration, and Weng Tiehui, Vice Mayor of Shanghai, signing an agreement on strategic cooperation, April 12, 2017. On October 19, 2017, SHU Institute of Cultural Heritage Protection and the Alliance on Technological Innovations of Cultural Heritage Along the Silk Road were established.

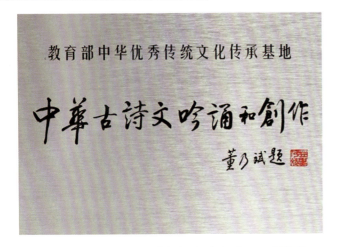

2018年11月28日,"中华古诗文吟诵和创作"获批教育部中华优秀传统文化传承基地

Institute of Recitation and Creation of Ancient Chinese Poetry, enlisted as the Chinese Excellent Cultural Heritage Base by the Ministry of Education, November 28, 2018

2019年12月25日,举行新结构经济学研究院成立揭牌仪式,林毅夫任名誉院长、名誉教授,校党委书记成旦红、副校长聂清出席

The unveiling ceremony of the Institute of New Structural Economics of SHU, Lin Yifu serving as Honorary Dean, December 25, 2019

2020年1月,"国家语言文字推广基地"挂牌成立

SHU enlisted as the National Language Promotion Base, January 2020

（三）重大奖项
Key Awards

1. 理工科　Key Awards in Science and Engineering

国家级重大奖项
National Key Awards

年度	奖项类别	项目名称	名次	获奖者
1995	国家自然科学奖	非线性偏微分方程的差分方法和谱方法及应用	三等奖	郭本瑜（上海大学）
1995	国家科技进步奖	三米激光丝杠动态测量仪	三等奖	陈明仪（上海大学）　孙麟治（上海大学）　程维明（上海大学）　刘继发（上海大学）　陆林海（上海大学）
2006	国家自然科学奖	珠江三角洲环境中毒害有机污染物研究	二等奖	傅家谟（上海大学）　张干　麦碧娴　王新明　吴明红（上海大学）
2012	国家科技进步奖	碳／碳复合材料工艺技术装备及应用	二等奖	孙晋良（上海大学）　任慕苏（上海大学）　张家宝（上海大学）　李红（上海大学）　潘剑峰（上海大学）　陈来（上海大学）　周春节（上海大学）　沈建荣（上海大学）　凌宝民（上海大学）　杨敏（上海大学）
2012	国家科技进步奖	军用先进核动力堆用锆合金关键基础研究	二等奖	周邦新（上海大学）　王丛林　王晓敏　刘庆　李中奎　龙冲生　伍晓勇　姚美意（上海大学）　邱少宇　周军
2012	国家科技进步奖	数字视频编解码技术国家标准AVS与产业化应用	二等奖	高文　黄铁军　虞露　何芸　马思伟　陈熙霖　王国中（上海大学）　张爱东（上海大学）　张恩阳　梁凡
2012	国家自然科学奖	低维纳米功能材料与器件原理的物理力学研究	二等奖	郭万林　胡海岩　张田忠（上海大学）　郭宇锋　王立锋

（续表）

年度	奖项类别	项目名称	名次	获奖者
2016	国家技术发明奖	复杂岛礁水域无人自主测量关键技术及装备	二等奖	谢少荣（上海大学） 罗均（上海大学） 彭艳（上海大学） 蒲华燕（上海大学） 狄伟 赵建国
2017	国家自然科学奖	高速运动刚柔相互作用系统非线性建模与振动分析	二等奖	杨绍普 陈立群（上海大学） 李韶华 申永军 丁虎（上海大学）
2017	国家技术发明奖	脉冲磁致振荡连铸方坯凝固均质化技术	二等奖	翟启杰（上海大学） 龚永勇（上海大学） 李仁兴（上海大学） 周湛 仲红刚（上海大学） 徐智帅（上海大学）
2018	国家自然科学奖	石墨烯微结构调控及其表面效应研究	二等奖	吴明红（上海大学） 潘登余（上海大学） 曹傲能（上海大学） 涂育松（上海大学） 王海芳（上海大学）
2018	国家科技进步奖	海气界面环境弱目标特性高灵敏度微波探测关键技术及装备	二等奖	陈希 魏艳强 陈雪（上海大学） 毛科峰 李浩 张丰 张云海 杨毅（上海大学） 任迎新 刘媛媛（上海大学）
2018	国家技术发明奖	基于M3组织调控的钢铁材料基础理论研究与高性能钢技术	二等奖	董瀚（上海大学） 翁宇庆 曹文全 孙新军 王存宇 谢振家
2019	国家技术发明奖	复杂振动的宽域近零超稳抑制技术与装置	二等奖	陈学东 蒲华燕（上海大学） 罗欣 姜伟 李小清 曾理湛
2019	国家科技进步奖	考古现场脆弱性文物临时固型提取及其保护技术	二等奖	罗宏杰（上海大学） 周铁 容波 韩向娜 房强 黄晓（上海大学） 张秉坚 姜标 王春燕 李伟东
备注：1.按获奖排名先后排列；2.外单位获奖人员不列单位				

部分获奖者
Some Prize Winners

陈明仪教授领衔的"三米激光丝杠动态测量仪"项目获1995年度国家科技进步奖三等奖

Professor Chen Mingyi's team winning the Third Prize of the 1995 National Prize for Progress in Science and Technology

傅家谟教授领衔的"珠江三角洲环境中毒害有机污染物研究"获2006年度国家自然科学奖二等奖

Professor Fu Jiamo's team winning the Second Prize of the 2006 National Prize for Natural Sciences

张田忠教授参与的"低维纳米功能材料与器件原理的物理力学研究"获2012年度国家自然科学奖二等奖

Professor Zhang Tianzhong, together with other team members, winning the Second Prize of the 2012 National Natural Science Award

周邦新院士领衔的"军用先进核动力堆用锆合金关键基础 研究"和孙晋良院士(左)领衔的"碳/碳复合材料工艺技术装备及应用"获2012年度国家科技进步奖

Academician Zhou Bangxin's (right) team and Academician Sun Jinliang's (left) team winning the 2012 National Prize for Progress in Science and Technology

谢少荣(左二)教授领衔的"复杂岛礁水域无人自主测量关键技术及装备"获2016年度国家技术发明奖二等奖

Professor Xie Shaorong's (second from left) team winning the Second Prize of the 2016 National Prize for Technological Invention

翟启杰教授（中）领衔的"脉冲磁致振荡连铸方坯凝固均质化技术"获2017年度国家技术发明奖二等奖

Professor Zhai Qijie's (middle) team winning the Second Prize of the 2017 National Prize for Technological Invention

陈立群（左）、丁虎教授参与的"高速运动刚柔相互作用系统非线性建模与振动分析"获2017年度国家自然科学奖二等奖

Professor Chen Liqun (left), Professor Ding Hu, together with other team members, winning the Second Prize of the 2017 National Natural Science Award

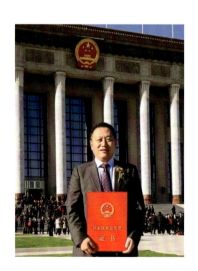

董瀚教授领衔的"基于M3组织调控的钢铁材料基础理论研究与高性能钢技术"获2018年度国家技术发明奖二等奖

Professor Dong Han's team winning the Second Prize of the 2018 National Prize for Technological Invention

吴明红教授领衔的"石墨烯微结构调控及其表面效应研究"获2018年度国家自然科学奖二等奖

Professor Wu Minghong's team winning the Second Prize of the 2018 National Natural Science Award

陈雪副教授参与的"海气界面环境弱目标特性高灵敏度微波探测关键技术及装备"项目获2018年度国家科技进步奖二等奖

Associate Professor Chen Xue, together with other team members, winning the Second Prize of the 2018 National Prize for Progress in Science and Technology

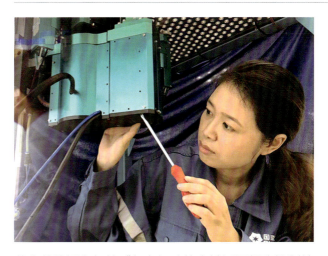

蒲华燕教授参与的"复杂振动的宽域近零超稳抑制技术与装置"获 2019 年度国家技术发明奖二等奖

Professor Pu Huayan, together with other team members, winning the Second Prize of the 2019 National Prize for Technological Invention

罗宏杰教授团队的"考古现场脆弱性文物临时固型提取及其保护技术"获 2019 年度国家科技进步奖二等奖

Professor Luo Hongjie's team winning the Second Prize of the 2019 National Prize for Progress in Science and Technology

2. 文科　Key Projects in Humanities and Social Sciences

2020 年第八届教育部高等学校科学研究优秀成果奖（人文社会科学）一等奖获得者

The Outstanding Achievement Award for Scientific Research in Institutions of Higher Education (Humanities and Social Sciences) (The First Prize), 2020

李友梅教授等所著的《新时期加强社会组织建设研究》获第八届一等奖；2015 年领衔的《当代中国社会建设的公共性困境及其超越》获第七届二等奖

Professor Li Youmei et al., authors of *A Study on Strengthening the Construction of Social Organizations in the New Era*, winning the First Prize, 2020; Professor Li Youmei et al., authors of "The Publicity Dilemma in the Social Construction of Contemporary China and How It Can Be Transcended," winning the Second Prize, 2015

金波教授等所著的《数字档案馆生态系统研究》

Professor Jin Bo et al., authors of *Ecosystem of Digital Archives*

2015年第七届教育部高等学校科学研究优秀成果奖（人文社会科学）二等奖获得者
The Outstanding Achievement Award for Scientific Research in Institutions of Higher Education (Humanities and Social Sciences) (The Second Prize), 2015

仇立平教授等所著的《文化资本与社会地位获得——基于上海市的实证研究》

Professor Qiu Liping et al., authors of "Cultural Capital and Status Attainment: An Empirical Study Based in Shanghai"

董丽敏教授所著的《性别、语境与书写的政治》

Professor Dong Limin, author of *Gender, Context, and Politics of Writing*

邵炳军教授等所著的《春秋文学系年辑证（全四册）》

Professor Shao Bingjun et al., authors of *Compilation and Almanacs of Literature of Spring and Autumn Period (four volumes)*

2020年第八届教育部高等学校科学研究优秀成果奖（人文社会科学）二等奖获得者
The Outstanding Achievement Award for Scientific Research in Institutions of Higher Education (Humanities and Social Sciences) (The Second Prize), 2020

曾军教授所著的《西方文论对中国经验的阐释及其相关问题》

Professor Zeng Jun, author of "Interpretations of the 'Chinese Experience' in Western Literary Theories"

饶龙隼教授所著的《元末明初大转变时期东南文坛格局及文学走向研究》

Professor Rao Longsun, author of *Study of Pattern of Southeast Literary Circles and Literary Trend During the Period of Great Transformation in the Late Yuan and Early Ming Dynasties*

丁治民教授所著的《〈永乐大典〉小学书辑佚与研究》

Professor Ding Zhimin, author of *Compilation and Study of Ancient Lexicography in the Yongle Encyclopedia*

张勇安教授所著的《科学与政治之间：美国医学会与毒品管制源起（1847—1973）》

Professor Zhang Yong'an, author of *Between Science and Politics: The American Medical Association and the Origins of Drug Control (1847-1973)*

郭丹彤教授所著的《古代埃及象形文字文献译注（上、中、下卷）》

Professor Guo Dantong, author of *Chinese Translation and Commentary of the Hieroglyphic Documents of Ancient Egypt (3 volumes)*

孙伟平教授所著的《事实与价值——休谟问题及其解决尝试（修订本）》

Professor Sun Weiping, author of *Facts and Values: Hume's Problem and Its Solution (Revised Edition)*

肖瑛教授所著的《从"国家与社会"到"制度与生活"：中国社会变迁研究的视角转换》

Professor Xiao Ying, author of *"From 'State and Society' to 'Institutions and Life': A Shift in the Study of Social Change in China"*

郭亮副教授所著的《十七世纪欧洲与晚明地图交流》

Associate Professor Guo Liang, author of *Cartography Exchange Between Europe and China in the 17th Century*

镇璐教授所著的《集装箱港口运作管理优化问题研究》

Professor Zhen Lu, author of *Research on Optimization of Container Port Operation Management*

教育部高等学校科学研究优秀成果奖（人文社会科学）三等奖和青年奖获得者
The Outstanding Achievement Award for Scientific Research in Institutions of Higher Education (Humanities and Social Sciences) (The Third Prize and the Youth Award)

名　次	届　别	项目名称	学　院	获奖者	类　别
三等奖	2006年第四届	民众评价论	社科学院	陈新汉	著作类
三等奖	2006年第四届	中国的利率管制与利率市场化	商管学院	王国松	论文类
三等奖	2006年第四届	中国社会总资金流量和结构监控	商管学院	陈湛匀	著作类
三等奖	2009年第五届	我国流域跨界水污染纠纷协调机制研究：以淮河流域为例	管理学院	赵来军	著作类
三等奖	2009年第五届	权威评价论	社科学院	陈新汉	著作类
三等奖	2009年第五届	中国传播思想史（共四卷）	影视学院	金冠军　戴元光	著作类
三等奖	2009年第五届	当代西方传媒制度	影视学院	郑　涵　金冠军	著作类
三等奖	2012年第六届	从财富分配到风险分配：中国社会结构重组的一种新路径	社会学院	李友梅	论文类
三等奖	2012年第六届	城市新移民社会融合的结构、现状与影响因素分析	社会学院	张文宏　雷开春	论文类
三等奖	2012年第六届	传教士中医观的变迁	文学院	陶飞亚	论文类
三等奖	2015年第七届	电影论——对电影学的总体思考（上下册）	影视学院	蓝　凡	著作类
三等奖	2020年第八届	泛娱乐时代的影游产业互动融合	上海电影学院	聂　伟　杜　梁	论文类
三等奖	2020年第八届	城市白领新移民研究	社会学院	张文宏　雷开春	著作类
青年奖	2020年第八届	儒家的如何是好	社科学部	朱　承	著作类
青年奖	2020年第八届	当代中国社会组织的制度环境与发展	社会学院	黄晓春	论文类

艺术类奖项
Awards in Art

2004年12月，美术学院教师秦一峰、岑沫石的作品"南京路下沉广场方案"获第十届全国美术艺术展金奖

"Sinking Square Plan for Nanjing Road," by Qin Yifeng and Cen Moshi, teachers of Shanghai Academy of Fine Arts, winning the Gold Award of the Tenth National Art Exhibition, December 2004

2004年12月，美术学院教师丁蓓莉的作品"在另一个季节"获第十届全国美术艺术展银奖

"In a Different Season," by Ding Beili, a teacher of Shanghai Academy of Fine Arts, winning the Silver Award of the Tenth National Art Exhibition, December 2004

2009年，美术学院教授李超所著的《中国早期油画史》获首届"中国美术奖·理论评论奖"

A History of Early Period Oil Painting in China, by Professor Li Chao, winning the First "Theoretical Review Award of Chinese Fine Arts," 2009

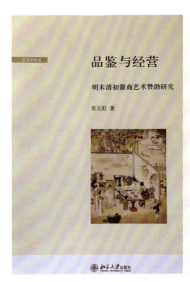 

2014年11月，美术学院教授张长虹所著的《品鉴与经营——明末清初徽商艺术赞助研究》获第二届"中国美术奖·理论评论奖"三等奖

Appreciation and Management by Professor Zhang Changhong winning the Third Prize of the Second "Theoretical Review Award of Chinese Fine Arts," 2014

2012年,电影学院教师陈志宏创作的《大闹天宫》(3D版)在夏威夷国际电影节上获"最佳美术指导奖",在第八届中国国际动漫节2012年"金猴奖"评选中获"中国动画电影优胜奖";《犟驴小红军》获中国文化艺术政府奖第三届动漫奖"最佳动漫作品奖"

The Monkey King: Uproar in Heaven, directed by Chen Zhihong, a teacher of Shanghai Film Academy, winning Outstanding Achievement in Animation at the Hawaii International Film Festival and The "Merit Award of 'Golden Monkey-King Award' China Animated Feature" of the Eighth Chinese International Animation Festival, 2012; Chen's The Stubborn Little Soldier winning "Best Animation" in the Third Chinese Government Award in Culture and Art, 2012

2014年12月,美术学院教师王秦创作的《欢乐颂》在第十二届全国美术作品展览中获"中国美术奖·创作奖"铜奖

"Ode to Joy," by Wang Qin, a teacher of Shanghai Academy of Fine Arts, winning the Bronze Prize of "Creation Award of Chinese Fine Arts" in the 12th National Fine Arts Exhibition, 2014

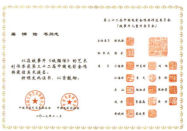

电影学院教师屠楠、陆苇凭电影《妖猫传》获2018年第12届亚洲电影大奖最佳美术指导、2019年第32届中国电影金鸡奖最佳美术奖

The movie Legend of the Demon Cat, winning Tu Nan and Lu Wei, teachers of Shanghai Film Academy, the "Best Production Design" prize at the 12th Asian Film Awards, 2018, and the "Best Art Direction" prize at the 32nd China Golden Rooster Awards, 2019

（四）重大项目
Key Projects

1. 理工科
Key Projects in Science and Engineering

2012年9月12日，上海市科委组织专家对任忠鸣教授主持的重大专项课题"高温合金叶片制造技术研究"进行验收

Evaluation conference on the key project "Research on Manufacturing Technology of Superalloy Blade," directed by Professor Ren Zhongming, 2012

2016年10月12日，吴晓春教授主持的"十三五"国家重点研发计划之"高性能工模具钢及应用"项目启动会暨高端工模具钢产业联盟和高端工模具钢"产—销—研—用"示范平台成立签约仪式在上海召开

The launching meeting of the national key project "High Performance Mold Steel and Application" directed by Professor Wu Xiaochun and the signing ceremony of the establishment of "Production-Sales-Research-Application" Demonstration Platform, 2016

2016年12月5日，钟云波研究员主持的"十三五"国家重点研发计划重点项目"高性能工模具钢及应用"项目课题——"工模具钢冶金过程的共性技术"启动会在济源市中原特钢股份有限公司召开

The launching meeting of the national key project "Common Technology of Mold Steel Metallurgical Process" directed by Researcher Zhong Yunbo, 2016

2017年1月12日，任忠鸣教授主持的国家自然科学基金重大项目"电磁场影响冶金相变过程机理"启动会在学校召开

The launching meeting of the National Natural Science Foundation of China (NSFC) project "Study on Mechanism of Metallurgical Phase Transition Under the Action of Electromagnetic Field" directed by Professor Ren Zhongming, 2017

2017年10月21日，张建华教授主持的国家重点研发计划"战略性先进电子材料"重点专项项目"柔性基板材料关键技术开发与应用示范"项目启动会在上海召开

The launching meeting of the national key project "Development and Application of Key Technologies of Flexible Substrate Materials" directed by Professor Zhang Jianhua, 2017

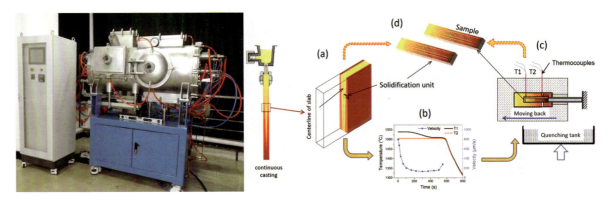

2018年3月13日，翟启杰教授主持的国家自然科学基金委重大仪器专项"连铸坯枝晶生长热模拟试验机"在北京通过验收，专家组对该项目原创的热模拟技术给予A级评价（左图为连铸坯枝晶生长热模拟试验机，右图为铸坯枝晶生长热模拟方法原理图）

The NSFC project "Continuous Casting Billet Dendrite Growth Thermal Simulation Testing Machine," directed by Professor Zhai Qijie, passing the acceptance review, 2018 (the left is the thermal simulation testing machine for dendrite growth of continuous casting billet; and the right is the schematic diagram of the thermal simulation method for dendrite growth of casting billet)

2018年3月,刘文光教授领衔的核电站隔震减震工程技术研究中心团队承担2017—2020年度国家重大科技专项课题"大型先进压水堆及高温气冷堆核电站"

The national project "Large Advanced Pressurized Water Reactor and High Temperature Gas-Cooled Reactor Nuclear Power Plant" undertaken by Professor Liu Wenguang and his team

2018年9月15日,钱权研究员主持的国家重点研发计划材料基因工程关键技术与支撑平台专项"材料基因工程专用数据库平台建设与示范应用"项目启动会在上海召开

The launching meeting of the national key project "The Special Data Platform for Material Genetic Engineering" directed by Researcher Qian Quan, 2018

2018年12月29日,张文清教授主持的国家重点研发计划"跨尺度高通量自动流程功能材料集成计算算法和软件"项目2018年度会议在国家超级计算无锡中心召开。该项目于2017年10月14日启动

The annual meeting of the national key project "Cross-Scale High-Throughput Automatic Process Functional Materials Integrated Computing Algorithms and Software" directed by Professor Zhang Wenqing, 2018

2019年1月16日，国家自然科学基金委与金砖国家科技创新框架计划"多铁材料的电学和磁学性质"项目启动会在学校召开

The launching meeting of "Electrical and Magnetic Properties of Multiferroic Materials," an NSFC project and The BRICS Science and Technology Innovation Framework Plan, 2019

2019年4月25日，张东升教授主持的国家重点研发计划"重大科学仪器设备开发"重点专项"大型设施挠度非接触测量仪"项目实施方案论证暨技术交流会在学校召开

The conference on the national key project "Large Facility Deflection Non-contact Measuring Instrument" directed by Professor Zhang Dongsheng, 2019

2019年，谢少荣教授牵头申报的"复杂海况无人艇集群控制理论与应用"项目获批国家自然科学基金委信息科学部人工智能代码（F06）首个重大项目

The national project "Theory and Application of Complex Marine Unmanned Surface Vehicle Cluster Control" directed by Professor Xie Shaorong, 2019

2. 文科 Key Projects in Humanities and Social Sciences

国家社科基金重大项目
Key Projects Funded by the National Office of Philosophy and Social Sciences

序号	部门	负责人	项目名称	项目类别	项目编号
1	校办	李友梅	新时期社会协调机制建设问题研究	重大项目	05&ZD030
2	文学院	张文宏	社会分层流动的和谐互动研究	重大项目	11&ZD035
3	文学院	张海东	社会质量与和谐社会建设研究	重大项目	11&ZD148
4	文学院	陶飞亚	汉语基督教文献书目的整理与研究	重大项目	12&ZD128
5	文学院	谢维扬	中国国家起源研究的理论与方法	重大项目	12&ZD133
6	文学院	张寅彭	清代诗话全编	重大项目	12&ZD160
7	文学院	徐有威	"小三线"建设资料的整理与研究	重大项目	13&ZD097
8	社会发展研究院	于逢春	中国疆域最终奠定的路径与模式研究	重大项目	15ZDB028
9	文学院	董乃斌	中国诗歌叙事传统研究	重大项目	15ZDB067
10	社会学院	蒋耒文	"一带一路"倡议下的中国和沿线国家国际人口迁移研究	重大项目	16ZDA088
11	文学院	邵炳军	《诗经》与礼制研究	重大项目	16ZDA172
12	文学院	曾军	20世纪西方文论中的中国问题研究	重大项目	16ZDA194
13	上海电影学院	许正林	当代中国文化国际影响力的生成研究	重大项目	16ZDA219
14	社会学院	李友梅	当代中国转型社会学理论范式创新研究	重大项目	17ZDA112
15	文学院	吕建昌	三线建设工业遗产保护与创新利用的路径研究	重大项目	17ZDA207
16	文学院	饶龙隼	中国古代文学制度研究	重大项目	17ZDA238
17	文学院	姚蓉	明清唱和诗词集整理与研究	重大项目	17ZDA258
18	文学院	江时学	"人类命运共同体"思想的历史学研究	重大项目	18ZDA170
19	文学院	郭丹彤	古代埃及新王国时期行政文献整理研究	重大项目	18ZDA206
20	文学院	张勇安	《国际禁毒史》(多卷本)	重大项目	18ZDA215

（续表）

序号	部门	负责人	项目名称	项目类别	项目编号
21	文学院	杨绪容	明清戏曲评点整理与研究	重大项目	18ZDA252
22	文学院	王卓华	全清诗歌总集文献整理与研究	重大项目	18ZDA254
23	马克思主义学院	孙伟平	人工智能前沿问题的马克思主义哲学研究	重大项目	19ZDA018
24	文学院	潘守永	民族大调查的学术回顾、文献整理和当代价值研究	重大项目	19ZDA174
25	文学院	廖大伟	中国近代纺织史资料整理与研究	重大项目	19ZDA213
26	文学院	程恭让	"一带一路"佛教交流史	重大项目	19ZDA239
27	文学院	宁镇疆	出土简帛文献与古书形成问题研究	重大项目	19ZDA250
28	文学院	尹楚兵	东林学派文献整理与文献研究	重大项目	19ZDA258
29	文学院	丁治民	东亚汉字文化圈《切韵》文献集成与研究	重大项目	19ZDA316
30	图书情报档案系	金波	数字档案馆生态系统治理研究	重大项目	19ZDA342
31	上海美术学院	李超	中国近现代美术国际交流文献研究	重大项目	20ZD15
32	文学院	刘旭光	中国近代以来艺术中的审美理论话语研究	重大项目	20ZD28

教育部哲学社会科学研究重大课题

Key Projects Funded by the Ministry of Education

序号	部门	负责人	项目名称	项目类别	项目编号/年份
1	社科学院	安维复	"邓小平理论和'三个代表'重要思想概论""精彩一门课"全程教学示范片研究制作	高校思想政治理论课专项	2004
2	商管学院	陈宪	中国现代服务经济理论与发展战略研究	重大攻关项目	06JZD0018
3	文学院	李友梅	新时期加强社会组织建设研究	重大攻关项目	11JZD027
4	社会学院	范明林	推进以保障和改善民生为重点的社会体制改革研究	重大攻关项目	13JZD025
5	文学院	郭长刚	土耳其内政外交政策与"一带一路"倡议研究	重大攻关项目	17JZD036
6	社科学部	王天恩	人工智能的哲学思考研究	重大攻关项目	18JZD013

2011年11月,张文宏教授主持的国家社科基金重大项目"社会分层流动的和谐互动研究"开题报告会在学校召开

The proposal conference on "The Harmonious Interaction of Social Stratification and Mobility" directed by Professor Zhang Wenhong, 2011

2012年3月,李友梅教授主持的教育部哲学社会科学重大攻关项目"新时期加强社会组织建设研究"开题报告会在学校召开

The proposal conference on "A Study on Strengthening the Construction of Social Organization in the New Era" directed by Professor Li Youmei, 2012

2012年12月,陶飞亚教授主持的国家社科基金重大项目"汉语基督教文献书目的整理与研究"开题会在学校召开

The proposal conference on "The Christian Literature in Chinese" directed by Professor Tao Feiya, 2012

2017年3月,曾军教授主持的国家社科基金重大项目"20世纪西方文论中的中国问题研究"开题报告会在学校召开

The proposal conference on "The 'China Questions' in Western Literary Theories in the 20th Century" directed by Professor Zeng Jun, 2017

2017年7月，董乃斌教授主持的国家社科基金重大项目"中国诗歌叙事传统研究"中期成果汇报推进会在学校召开

The progress review conference on "Narrative Tradition of Chinese Poetry" directed by Professor Dong Naibin, 2017

2018年1月，饶龙隼教授主持的国家社科基金重大项目"中国古代文学制度研究"开题报告会在学校召开

The proposal conference on "System of Chinese Ancient Literature" directed by Professor Rao Longsun, 2018

2018年3月，郭长刚教授主持的教育部哲学社会科学研究重大课题攻关项目"土耳其内政外交政策与'一带一路'倡议研究"开题报告会在学校召开

The proposal conference on "Turkish Internal and Foreign Policy and 'Belt & Road' Initiative" directed by Professor Guo Changgang, 2018

2018年6月，邵炳军教授主持的国家社科基金重大项目"《诗经》与礼制研究"中期预评估暨项目推进会在学校召开

The progress review conference on "*The Book of Songs* and Etiquette" directed by Professor Shao Bingjun, 2018

2019年1月,王天恩教授主持的教育部哲学社会科学研究重大课题攻关项目"人工智能的哲学思考研究"开题研讨会在学校召开

The proposal conference on "Artificial Intelligence from Philosophical Perspectives" directed by Professor Wang Tian'en, 2019

2019年3月,郭丹彤教授主持的国家社科基金重大项目"古代埃及新王国时期行政文献整理研究"、张勇安教授主持的国家社科基金重大项目"《国际禁毒史》(多卷本)"、江时学教授主持的国家社科基金重大项目"'人类命运共同体'思想的历史学研究"开题报告会在学校召开

The proposal conferences on book project "The Administrative Documents During the New Kingdom of Ancient Egypt" directed by Professor Guo Dantong, book project *The International History of Drug Control* (Multi-volume)" directed by Professor Zhang Yong'an, and book project "A Historic Perspective of the Concept of Building a Community of Common Destiny for All Mankind" directed by Professor Jiang Shixue, 2019

2020年7月17日,孙伟平教授主持的国家社科基金重大项目"人工智能前沿问题的马克思主义哲学研究"开题研讨会在学校召开

The proposal conference on "The Frontiers of Artificial Intelligence from the Perspective of Marxist Philosophy" directed by Professor Sun Weiping, 2020

（五）重要成果
Key Achievements

1997年，黄宏嘉院士在国际上首次提出并制出宽带光纤波片，被贝尔实验室命名为黄氏波片

"Huang Wave Plate," developed by Academician Huang Hongjia, 1997

2004年，黄宏嘉院士领衔的课题组制成国内第一台全光纤大电流互感器并成功在南汇变电站挂网

The first All-Fiber Large Current Transformer in China, developed by Academician Huang Hongjia and his team, 2004

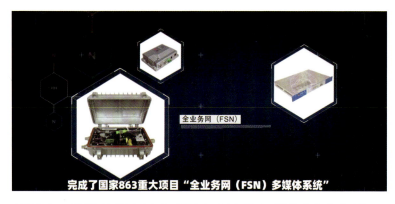

1999年，汪敏教授主持完成国家863重大项目"全业务网（FSN）多媒体系统"

The national key project "Multimedia System of Full Service Network," completed by Professor Wang Min, 1999

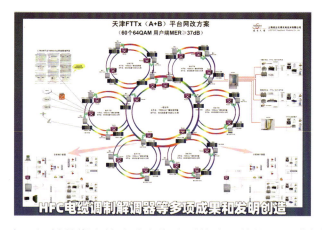

2000年，汪敏教授主持完成上海市科技成果转化项目"电缆调制解调器的产业化研究"，研制出我国第一代DOCSIS电缆调制解调器和ADSL调制解调器

China's first-generation DOCSIS Cable Modem and ADSL Modem, developed by Professor Wang Min, 2000

3D 视频系统课题组承担"上海世博会中国馆 3D 自由视点电视应用系统"展项，该系统由"森林碳汇"低碳展和"希望大地"湿地展两组展项组成
"The 3D Free View TV Application System of the China Pavilion at the Shanghai World Expo," undertaken by the 3D Video System Research Team of SHU

2013 年 6 月 5 日，《人民日报》报道《首艘自主无人测量艇南海巡航》
People's Daily reported on "The First Autonomous Unmanned Surface Vehicle Cruises in the South China Sea," June 5, 2013

无人艇在南极罗斯海探测
Unmanned Surface Vehicle exploring Ross Sea in Antarctica

2016年10月,上海大学精海系列无人艇参加中央军委装备发展部、教育部、工业和信息化部、国防科工局、全国工商联合举办的第二届军民融合发展高技术成果展,全国共21所高校受邀参加。

In October 2016, the Jinghai Unmanned Surface Vehicle of SHU was exhibited at the second High-Tech Military-Civilian Integrated Development Achievements Exhibition. A total of 21 Chinese universities were invited to participate in the exhibition.

2016年10月19日,中共中央总书记、国家主席、中央军委主席习近平与中共中央政治局常委、中共中央政治局委员、中央书记处书记、国务委员以及中央军委委员一同参观无人艇展位。(《习近平等参观第二届军民融合发展高技术成果展》,《人民日报》2016年10月20日)

On October 19, 2016, President Xi Jinping, accompanied by the members of the Standing Committee of the Political Bureau of the CPC Central Committee, members of the Political Bureau of the CPC Central Committee, members of the CPC Central Committee Secretariat, State Councilors, and members of the Central Military Commission, visited the SHU booth of unmanned surface vehicle. (Reported by *People's Daily*, October 20, 2016)

2016年10月,中共中央政治局委员、国务院副总理汪洋在展场听取上海大学精海无人艇团队汇报
Vice Premier Wang Yang listening to the report of SHU Jinghai Unmanned Surface Vehicle team during the exhibition, October 2016

2015年3月，宋任涛教授实验室在玉米蛋白质研究上取得重要进展，相关研究成果在美国植物学学术期刊《植物细胞》上发表

Professor Song Rentao and his team members making crucial progress in the study of maize protein and publishing the findings in *Plant Cell*, March 2015

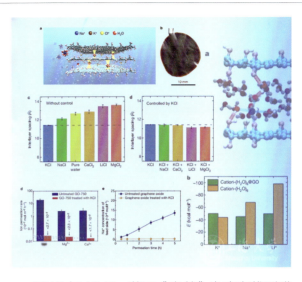

2017年10月，英国《自然》杂志在线刊登吴明红教授团队石墨烯研究领域成果

Professor Wu Minghong and her team publishing the new findings of graphene in *Nature*, October 2017

2018年3月，马克·沃勒教授等在英国《自然》杂志上发表论文

Professor Mark P. Waller et al., publishing an article in *Nature*, March 2018

2018年8月，曹世勋教授团队在凝聚态磁性系统中发现了第一个迪克协同作用的实例，该项成果在美国《科学》杂志上发表

Professor Cao Shixun and his team publishing the first article in *Science* in the field of Dicke cooperativity for SHU, August 2018

（六）学术期刊与图书出版
Publication of Journals and Books

《应用数学和力学（英文版）》创办于1980年，创刊人为中国近代力学的创始人之一钱伟长院士，由上海大学和中国力学学会主办、国际出版公司施普林格负责全球发行。1990年起期刊被EI数据库全文收录，1997年起被SCI数据库收录，是国内最早被SCI和EI收录的应用数学和力学类期刊，入选"2018年中国最具国际影响力学术期刊"

Applied Mathematics and Mechanics (English Edition), founded by Academician Qian Weichang in 1980, is sponsored by SHU and the Chinese Society of Mechanics and distributed worldwide by Springer. The journal has been indexed in EI database since 1990 and SCI database since 1997. In 2018, it was listed in the "Academic Journals with the Highest International Impact in China."

《社会》杂志入选"2019中国最具国际影响力学术期刊"

Chinese Journal of Sociology, listed in the "Academic Journals with the Highest International Impact in China," 2019

上海大学出版社成立于 1996 年 6 月,由钱伟长校长创办。图为出版社出版的部分国家级精品图书

National quality books published by Shanghai University Press, founded by Academician Qian Weichang in June 1996

七

教师队伍
Faculty and Staff

（一）中国科学院院士
Academicians of the Chinese Academy of Sciences

钱伟长（1955 年当选学部委员，后改称院士）
Qian Weichang (elected Member of the Chinese Academy of Sciences in 1955, later renamed Academician)

黄宏嘉（1980 年当选学部委员，后改称院士）
Huang Hongjia (elected Member of the Chinese Academy of Sciences in 1980, later renamed Academician)

刘高联（1999 年）
Liu Gaolian（1999）

张统一（2011 年）
Zhang Tongyi (2011)

刘昌胜（2017 年）
Liu Changsheng (2017)

（二）中国工程院院士
Academicians of the Chinese Academy of Engineering

徐匡迪（1995 年）
Xu Kuangdi (1995)

周邦新（1995 年）
Zhou Bangxin (1995)

孙晋良（1997 年）
Sun Jinliang (1997)

（三）终身教授　Tenured Professors

方明伦（2005年）
Fang Minglun（2005）

刘高联（2006年）
Liu Gaolian（2006）

周邦新（2006年）
Zhou Bangxin（2006）

徐匡迪（2006年）
Xu Kuangdi（2006）

黄宏嘉（2006年）
Huang Hongjia（2006）

孙晋良（2009年）
Sun Jinliang（2009）

董乃斌（2009年）
Dong Naibin（2009）

戴世强（2009年）
Dai Shiqiang（2009）

邓伟志（2011年）
Deng Weizhi（2011）

龚振邦（2011年）
Gong Zhenbang（2011）

董远达（2011年）
Dong Yuanda（2011）

周哲玮（2015年）
Zhou Zhewei（2015）

（四）双聘科学院院士
Double Employed Academicians of the Chinese Academy of Sciences

刘元方（1991年） 　周国治（1995年） 　方岱宁（2013年） 　周向宇（2013年）
Liu Yuanfang (1991) 　Zhou Guozhi (1995) 　Fang Daining (2013) 　Zhou Xiangyu (2013)

（五）双聘工程院院士
Double Employed Academicians of the Chinese Academy of Engineering

李三立（1995年） 　刘　玠（1997年） 　金翔龙（1997年） 　刘人怀（1999年）
Li Sanli (1995) 　Liu Jie (1997) 　Jin Xianglong (1997) 　Liu Renhuai (1999)

李德毅（1999 年）
Li Deyi (1999)

（六）外籍院士
Academicians of Non-Chinese Academies

钱伟长，1956 年当选波兰科学院外籍院士
Qian Weichang, elected Member of the Polish Academy of Sciences, 1956

徐匡迪，2003 年当选瑞典皇家工程院外籍院士、2006 年当选美国国家工程院外籍院士、俄罗斯工程科学院外籍院士
Xu Kuangdi, elected Member of the Royal Swedish Academy of Engineering, 2003, Member of the National Academy of Engineering in the US and the Academy of Engineering Sciences of the Russian Federation, 2006

吴明红，2008 年当选俄罗斯工程院外籍院士
Wu Minghong, elected Academician of the Academy of Engineering of the Russian Federation, 2008

张久俊，2017 年当选加拿大皇家科学院外籍院士
Zhang Jiujun, elected Member of the Royal Canadian Institute, 2017

（七）领军人物　Leading Figures

（国家"973计划"首席科学家，国家杰出青年科学基金获得者，万人计划领军人才，百千万人才工程国家级人选，长江学者特聘教授，教育部专业教学指导委员会负责人，等等）

罗宏杰　Luo Hongjie

董　瀚　Dong Han

敖　平　Ao Ping

吉永华　Ji Yonghua

任忠鸣　Ren Zhongming

赵春华　Zhao Chunhua

汪小帆　Wang Xiaofan

陈立群　Chen Liqun

高彦峰　Gao Yanfeng

顾　辉　Gu Hui

张田忠　Zhang Tianzhong

张新鹏　Zhang Xinpeng

谢少荣　Xie Shaorong

张建华　Zhang Jianhua

周　全　Zhou Quan

王　刚　Wang Gang

徐树公　Xu Shugong

张文宏　Zhang Wenhong

曾　军　Zeng Jun

钱晋武　Qian Jinwu

 程恭让 Cheng Gongrang
 施利毅 Shi Liyi
 孙伟平 Sun Weiping
 彭 晨 Peng Chen

 钟云波 Zhong Yunbo
 李友梅 Li Youmei
 金 波 Jin Bo
 吕 斌 Lü Bin

 顾 骏 Gu Jun

（八）外聘院长　Distinguished Non-track Deans

序 号	姓 名	部 门	职 务
1	李三立	计算机工程与科学学院	院长（1988年—2015年2月）
2	谢　晋	影视艺术与技术学院	院长（1995年4月—2008年10月）
3	匡定波	通信与信息工程学院	院长（1995年5月—2018年4月）
4	叶　辛	文学院	院长（1999年5月起，2015年改聘为名誉院长）
5	邱瑞敏	美术学院	院长（1999年9月—2011年4月）
6	庄松林	机电工程与自动化学院	院长（1999年起，2011年6月改聘为名誉院长）
7	沈学础	理学院	院长（2000年12月—2016年10月）
8	傅家谟	环境与化学工程学院	院长（2005年2月—2015年6月）
9	刘源张	原商管学院	院长（2005年5月—2010年10月）
10	沈四宝	法学院	院长（2008年10月—2016年9月）
11	李根喜	生命科学学院	院长（2008年11月—2011年10月）
12	斯晓夫	管理学院	院长（2008年5月—2011年12月）
13	尤建新	管理学院	院长（2011年12月—2017年11月）
14	丁建平	生命科学学院	院长（2014年9月—2017年8月）
15	郭毅可	计算机工程与科学学院	院长（2015年4月至今）
16	陈凯歌	上海电影学院	院长（2015年7月至今）
17	张久俊	理学院	院长（2016年10月至今）
18	董　瀚	材料科学与工程学院	院长（2016年1月至今）
19	贾樟柯	上海温哥华电影学院	院长（2016年6月至今）
20	王　勇	音乐学院	院长（2016年7月至今）
21	冯　远	上海美术学院	院长（2016年9月起，2020年5月改聘为名誉院长）
22	沈路一	生命科学学院	院长（2017年10月—2019年4月）
23	张　勇	环境与化学工程学院	院长（2017年2月至今）
24	刘宛予	中欧工程技术学院	执行院长（2018年1月起，2018年11月改聘为执行院长）
25	严三九	新闻传播学院	院长（2018年2月至今）
26	文学国	法学院	院长（2018年6月至今）
27	孙伟平	马克思主义学院	院长（2018年9月至今）
28	蒋为民	上海温哥华电影学院	执行院长（2019年4月至今）
29	赵春华	生命科学学院	院长（2019年12月至今）
30	古元冬	微电子学院	院长（2020年4月至今）
31	曾成钢	上海美术学院	院长（2020年5月至今）
32	刘人怀	管理学院	名誉院长（2020年8月至今）

（九）重要科研团队　Outstanding Research Teams

省部共建高品质特殊钢冶金与制备国家重点实验室（高温叶片科研团队）（先进钢铁材料技术国家工程研究中心南方实验基地科研团队）

Members of Superalloy Turbine Blade Research Team, the State Key Laboratory of Advanced Special Steel, Shanghai City and the Ministry of Education, also Research Group of Southern Experimental Base, National Engineering and Research Center for Advanced Steel Technology

省部共建高品质特殊钢冶金与制备国家重点实验室（模具钢科研团队）

Members of the Mold Steel Research Team, the State Key Laboratory of Advanced Special Steel, Shanghai City and the Ministry of Education

省部共建高品质特殊钢冶金与制备国家重点实验室（凝固中心科研团队）
Members of the Advanced Solidification Technology Team, the State Key Laboratory of Advanced Special Steel, Shanghai City and the Ministry of Education

特种光纤与光接入网省部共建教育部重点实验室科研团队
Members of the Key Laboratory of Specialty Fiber Optics and Optical Access Networks, Shanghai City and the Ministry of Education

新型显示技术及应用集成教育部重点实验室科研团队
Members of the research team of the Key Laboratory of Advanced Display and System Applications, Ministry of Education

有机复合污染控制工程教育部重点实验室科研团队
Members of the Key Laboratory of Organic Compound Pollution Control Engineering, Ministry of Education

材料复合与先进分散技术教育部工程研究中心科研团队
Members of the Engineering Research Center of Material Composition and Advanced Dispersion Technology, Ministry of Education

海洋智能无人系统装备教育部工程研究中心科研团队
Members of the Engineering Research Center of Marine Intelligent Unmanned Systems and Equipment, Ministry of Education

TFTLCD 关键材料及技术国家工程实验室科研团队
International Symposium on Advanced Display Materials and Devices, State Engineering Laboratory of TFTLCD, 2016

纳米复合功能材料国际科技合作基地科研团队
Members of the research team of the International Science and Technology Cooperation Base for Nanocomposite Functional Materials

社会学国家重点学科团队
Members of the national key discipline team of sociology

（十）国家荣誉称号获得者　Faculty Winning National Honors

荣誉称号	姓　名	年　份	颁奖单位
全国劳动模范	陈立群	2020 年	国务院
全国先进工作者并授予全国先进工作者奖章	曹家麟	2000 年	国务院
全国先进工作者并授予全国先进工作者奖章	孙晋良	2015 年	国务院
全国五一劳动奖章	孙晋良	2012 年	全国总工会
全国教育系统劳动模范并授予人民教师奖章	陈明仪	1995 年	教育部、人事部
全国教育系统劳动模范并授予全国教育系统劳动模范奖章	吴程里	1995 年	教育部、人事部
全国教育系统劳动模范并授予全国模范教师称号	曹家麟	1998 年	教育部、人事部
全国模范教师	吴明红	2004 年	教育部、人事部
全国模范教师	戴世强	2007 年	教育部、人事部
全国模范教师	陈立群	2009 年	教育部、人事部
全国模范教师	陈立群	2019 年	教育部、人力资源与社会保障部
全国优秀教师并授予全国优秀教师奖章	曹家麟	1995 年	教育部
全国优秀教师并授予全国优秀教师奖章	吴锡龙	1995 年	教育部
全国优秀教师、全国高校优秀思想政治理论课教师	李　梁	2009 年	教育部
全国优秀教育工作者	林振汉	2001 年	教育部

陈立群，2009、2019 年获"全国模范教师"称号，2020 年获"全国劳动模范"称号
Chen Liqun, winning the 2009 and 2019 National Model Teacher Award, and the 2020 National Model Worker Award

曹家麟，1995 年获"全国优秀教师"称号，1998 年获"全国教育系统劳动模范""全国模范教师"称号，2000 年获"全国先进工作者"称号
Cao Jialin, winning the 1995 National Outstanding Teacher Award, the 1998 National Model Worker in Education Award, the 1998 National Model Teacher Award, and the 2000 National Outstanding Worker Award

孙晋良，2012年获"全国五一劳动奖章"，2015年获"全国先进工作者"称号

Sun Jinliang, winning the 2012 National May 1st Medal and the 2015 National Outstanding Worker Award

陈明仪，1995年获"全国教育系统劳动模范"称号并获"人民教师奖章"

Chen Mingyi, winning the 1995 National Model Worker in Education Award and the People's Teacher Medal

吴程里，1995年获"全国教育系统劳动模范"称号并获"全国教育系统劳动模范奖章"

Wu Chengli, winning the 1995 National Model Worker in Education Award and Medal

吴明红，2004年获"全国模范教师"称号

Wu Minghong, winning the 2004 National Model Teacher Award

戴世强，2007年获"全国模范教师"称号

Dai Shiqiang, winning the 2007 National Model Teacher Award

吴锡龙，1995年获"全国优秀教师"称号并获"全国优秀教师奖章"

Wu Xilong, winning the 1995 National Outstanding Teacher Award and Medal

李梁，2009年获"全国优秀教师""全国高校优秀思想政治理论课教师"称号

Li Liang, winning the 2009 National Outstanding Teacher Award and the Award of National Outstanding Teacher of Ideological and Political Theory in Universities

林振汉，2001年获"全国优秀教育工作者"称号

Lin Zhenhan, winning the 2001 National Outstanding Educator Award

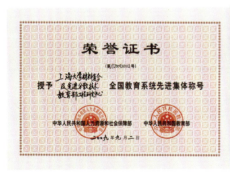

材料复合及先进分散技术教育部工程研究中心，2009年获"全国教育系统先进集体"称号

The Engineering Research Center of Material Composition and Advanced Dispersion Technology, Ministry of Education, winning the 2009 National Outstanding Unit in Education

无人艇教师团队（负责人罗均），2018年获"全国高校黄大年式教师团队"称号

The faculty of the Research Institute of Unmanned Surface Vehicle Engineering, winning the National Huang Danian-Style Teacher Team by the Ministry of Education, 2018

（十一）重要荣誉
Important Honors

钱伟长，1997年6月获何梁何利基金"科学与技术成就奖"
Qian Weichang, winning Science and Technology Progress Award by The Ho Leung Ho Lee Foundation, June 1997

黄宏嘉，1998年获何梁何利基金"科学与技术进步奖"
Huang Hongjia, winning Science and Technology Progress Award by The Ho Leung Ho Lee Foundation, 1998

徐匡迪，2006年获瑞典皇家北极星大十字司令官勋章，2007年获何梁何利基金"科学与技术进步奖"，2018年获第十二届"光华工程科技奖"
Xu Kuangdi, winning the Commander of the Royal Polaris Cross of Sweden, 2006, Science and Technology Progress Award by The Ho Leung Ho Lee Foundation, 2007, and the 12th Guanghua Engineering Technology Award, 2018

张统一，2018年获何梁何利基金"科学与技术进步奖"
Zhang Tongyi, winning Science and Technology Progress Award by The Ho Leung Ho Lee Foundation, 2018

孙晋良，1995年获光华科技基金奖二等奖，2006年获国家"杰出专业技术人才"称号，2008年获第七届"光华工程科技奖"
Sun Jinliang, winning the Second Prize of the Guanghua Science and Technology Fund, the 2006 National Outstanding Professional and Technical Personnel Award, and the 2008 Guanghua Engineering Science and Technology Award

陈明仪，1995年获光华科技基金奖三等奖
Chen Mingyi, winning the Third Prize of the Guanghua Science and Technology Fund, 1995

吴明红，2012年获第九届"光华工程科技奖"
Wu Minghong, winning the Ninth Guanghua Engineering Science and Technology Award, 2012

李友梅，2006年被授予法国骑士勋章
Li Youmei, winning the French Palm Knight Medal, 2006

李喜，2015年获法国科学院颁发"法中奖"
Li Xi, winning the Sino-French Prize by the French Academy of Sciences, 2015

孙菱，2017年获"法兰西共和国荣誉勋章"
Sun Ling, winning the Medal of Honor of the French Republic, 2017

澳大利亚籍专家杰弗里·雷默斯2017年获上海市"白玉兰纪念奖"
Australian academician Jeffery Reimers, winning the 2017 Shanghai Magnolia Silver Award

德国籍专家爱睿思·布洛威（右三）2018年获上海市"白玉兰纪念奖"
German Expert Iris Borowy (third from right), winning the 2018 Shanghai Magnolia Silver Award

英国籍教师王玫瑰2013年获上海市"白玉兰纪念奖"；2019年获上海市"白玉兰荣誉奖"，上海市市长应勇为其颁奖
British teacher Rosalind Stephanie Oliver, winning the 2013 Shanghai Magnolia Silver Award and the 2019 Shanghai Magnolia Gold Award

国际交流与合作

International Exchanges and Cooperations

（一）国际合作
Global Partners

学校致力于在全球范围内发展相互促进的教育联盟，与全球 51 个国家的近 200 所大学建立了校际合作伙伴关系。
SHU is committed to developing mutually productive alliances worldwide and has established university-level partnership with nearly 200 overseas universities in 51 countries.

阿根廷 Argentina（3）
阿根廷国家科学技术研究委员会
国立布宜诺斯艾利斯西北省大学
阿根廷国立艺术大学

阿塞拜疆 Azerbaijan（3）
阿塞拜疆国立经济大学
巴库国立大学
阿塞拜疆国立石油大学

埃及 Egypt（1）
十月六日大学

爱尔兰 Ireland（4）
科克大学
梅努斯大学
都柏林城市大学
科克理工学院

爱沙尼亚 Estonia（2）
塔尔图大学
塔林理工大学

奥地利 Austria（1）
库夫斯坦因应用科技大学

澳大利亚 Australia（11）
悉尼科技大学
麦考瑞大学
昆士兰大学
昆士兰科技大学
新南威尔士大学
斯威本科技大学
迪肯大学
拉筹伯大学
科廷大学
伍伦贡大学
西澳大利亚大学

巴基斯坦 Pakistan（1）
卡拉奇工商管理学院

巴林 Bahrain（1）
巴林大学

巴西 Brazil（3）
坎皮纳斯州立大学
圣保罗大学
巴西利亚大学

白俄罗斯 Belarus（2）
白俄罗斯国立大学
白俄罗斯国立信息技术无线电电子大学

比利时 Belgium（1）
根特大学

波兰 Poland（4）
华沙大学
波兹南技术大学
弗罗茨瓦夫经济大学
洛兹电影学院

丹麦 Denmark（1）
南丹麦大学

德国 Germany（8）
不来梅大学
卡塞尔大学
马克斯·普朗克固体物理化学研究所
奥登堡大学
卡尔斯鲁厄合作大学
德累斯顿应用科技大学
开姆尼茨工业大学
莱茵－瓦尔应用科技大学

多米尼加 Dominican Republic（1）
圣多明各理工大学

俄罗斯 Russia（3）
国家研究型高等经济大学
莫斯科国立大学
伊尔库茨克国立理工大学

法国 France（11）
格勒诺布尔阿尔卑斯大学
法国工程技术大学
里尔大学
里昂大学
雷恩第一大学
蒙彼利埃第三大学
勃艮第－弗朗什孔泰大学
雷恩高等商学院
诺曼底管理学院
法国 ESCE 对外贸易学院
洛林大学

芬兰 Finland（5）
奥卢大学
坦佩雷大学

芬兰北中部应用科技大学
拉普兰塔理工大学
瓦萨大学

古巴 Cuba（1）
古巴圣地亚哥东方大学

哈萨克斯坦 Kazakhstan（5）
哈萨克斯坦共和国欧亚大学
哈萨克斯坦国立大学
对外经济贸易大学
国际信息技术大学
苏莱曼－德米雷尔大学

韩国 Korea（11）
成均馆大学
梨花女子大学
庆熙大学
建国大学
国立釜山大学
中央大学
东国大学
全北国立大学
湖南大学
鲜文大学
首尔市立大学

荷兰 Netherlands（2）
海牙大学
埃因霍芬理工大学

加拿大 Canada（6）
多伦多大学
不列颠哥伦比亚大学
温哥华电影学院
西部大学
瑞尔森大学
阿卡迪亚大学

拉脱维亚 Latvia（2）
里加理工大学
里斯本商业、艺术和技术大学

立陶宛 Lithuania（1）
考纳斯理工大学

马来西亚 Malaysia（1）
拉曼大学

美国 United States（22）
宾夕法尼亚大学沃顿商学院
德克萨斯大学奥斯汀分校
德克萨斯大学里奥格兰德河谷分校
西北大学
莱斯大学
罗格斯大学
纽约州立大学石溪分校
纽约州立大学布法罗分校
纽约市立大学
明尼苏达大学双城分校
明尼苏达大学莫里斯分校
普渡大学
康奈尔大学
肯塔基大学
怀俄明大学
北卡罗莱纳州立大学
天普大学
内华达大学里诺分校
佛罗里达州立大学
乔治亚州立大学
卫斯理安学院
巴德学院

秘鲁 Peru（1）
秘鲁天主教大学

摩洛哥 Morocco（1）
戈迪·伊雅德大学

墨西哥 Mexico（2）
蒙特雷科技大学
普埃布拉美洲大学

葡萄牙 Portugal（2）
米尼奥大学
里斯本大学

日本 Japan（17）
早稻田大学
东北大学
千叶大学
近畿大学
关西学院大学
大阪市立大学
广岛市立大学
芝浦工业大学
大阪艺术大学
富山大学
大正大学

香川大学
创价大学
武藏野大学
神田外语大学
专修大学
东洋大学

瑞典 Sweden（4）
查尔姆斯理工大学
延雪平大学
瑞典西部大学
乌普萨拉大学

塞尔维亚 Serbia（1）
贝尔格莱德大学

圣马力诺 San Marino（1）
圣马力诺大学

斯洛伐克 Slovakia（1）
布拉迪斯拉发经济与公共管理学院

泰国 Thailand（4）
宋卡王子大学
西那瓦国际大学
清迈大学
玛希隆大学

土耳其 Turkey（4）
海峡大学
萨班哲大学
伊斯坦布尔科技大学
杰拉勒·拜亚尔大学

乌兹别克斯坦 Uzbekistan（4）
世界经济外交大学
国家美术设计学院
公共管理学院
塔什干国立经济大学

西班牙 Spain（2）
巴斯克大学
ESIC 商学院

希腊 Greece（2）
塞萨洛尼基亚里士多德大学
欧洲公法组织

新西兰 New Zealand（2）
奥克兰大学

奥塔哥大学

匈牙利 Hungary（1）
赛格德大学

亚美尼亚 Armenia（1）
叶里温国立大学

伊朗 Iran（1）
谢里夫理工大学

以色列 Israel（2）
海法大学
特拉维夫大学

意大利 Italy（9）
摩德纳·雷焦·艾米利亚大学
那不勒斯东方大学
特伦托大学
罗马大学
罗马第二大学
罗马第三大学
萨勒诺大学
米兰圣心天主教大学
都灵大学

印度 India（1）
韦洛尔理工大学

英国 United Kingdom（18）
牛津大学
剑桥大学
爱丁堡大学
利兹大学
贝尔法斯特女王大学
拉夫堡大学
萨塞克斯大学
皇家艺术学院
伦敦国王学院
曼彻斯特大学
曼彻斯特城市大学
肯特大学
布鲁内尔大学
埃塞克斯大学
利物浦约翰莫尔斯大学
思克莱德大学
利物浦大学
兰卡斯特大学

越南 Vietnam（1）
胡志明市国家大学

（二）合作办学与学术交流
Joint Education and Research

1994年7月，与澳大利亚悉尼科技大学合作建立的上海大学悉尼工商学院是国内首家通过国家认证的中外合作商学院。2020年2月，悉尼工商学院通过AACSB首次认证，为期五年，标志着上海大学悉尼工商学院成为全国首家本科层次通过AACSB认证的中外合作办学机构，上海大学成为首个通过AACSB国际认证的地方高校

SILC (Sydney Institute of Language and Commerce) Business School, co-founded by SHU and University of Technology Sydney (UTS) in 1994, is one of the earliest international joint business schools in China. In 2020, SILC earned AACSB accreditation after ratification by the IAC and Board of Directors, marking the enormous strides SILC has made in teaching, research, and social services and another big step toward becoming a globally-recognized business school. SILC is the first joint undergraduate program in China that has earned AACSB accreditation. Shanghai University is the first local university sponsored by local municipal government that has earned AACSB accreditation.

2004年10月12日，校党委书记、常务副校长方明伦出席上海大学—里尔科技大学学生交流协议签字仪式

The signing ceremony of student exchange agreement between SHU and Lille University of Science and Technology, October 12, 2004

2004年10月29日，举行中美—上海知识产权人才培训研讨会

Sino-America Intellectual Property Training Conference for Professionals, October 29, 2004

2012年6月4日，校长罗宏杰出席上海大学哈萨克斯坦研究中心成立揭牌仪式

The unveiling ceremony of Kazakhstan Research Center of SHU, June 4, 2012

2006年11月5日，全国政协副主席徐匡迪、法国工程院院长弗朗索瓦·吉诺出席上海大学中欧工程技术学院揭牌仪式

Sino-European School of Technology, SHU, unveiled by Xu Kuangdi, Vice Chairman of the National Committee of the CPPCC, and Francois Guinot, President of the French Academy of Engineering, November 5, 2006

2013年4月3日，副校长叶志明出席"上海大学—肯塔基大学全面合作推进会暨2+2双学位签字仪式"

The signing ceremony of a dual degree program held between SHU and University of Kentucky, April 3, 2013

2014年12月11日，举行"上海大学—牛津大学奥利尔学院—CBL国际教育"三方合作协议签署仪式

SHU signing a tripartite cooperation agreement with Oriel College, University of Oxford and CBL International Education, December 11, 2014

2015年12月14日，举行第二届"世界考古论坛·上海"，上海市市长杨雄、中国社会科学院院长王伟光、国家文物局局长刘玉珠等出席开幕式并致辞

The Second Shanghai Archaeology Forum at SHU, December 14, 2015. Yang Xiong, Mayor of Shanghai, Wang Weiguang, President of the Chinese Academy of Social Sciences, and Liu Yuzhu, Director of the National Cultural Heritage Administration, attended and addressed the ceremony.

2018年8月12日，举行第12届国际文化研究学会全球双年会

The "Crossroads in Cultural Studies 2018" at SHU, August 12, 2018

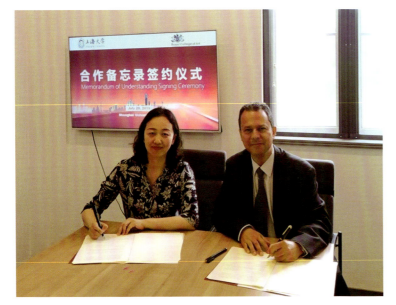

2019年7月20日，校党委副书记、副校长龚思怡代表学校与英国皇家艺术学院签署合作备忘录

The signing ceremony of a memorandum of cooperation between SHU and the British Royal College of Art, July 20, 2019

（三）师生海外交流
Overseas Programs for Faculty and Students

30名商科教师在沃顿商学院接受项目培训
Faculty of SHU business programs attending a training program at the Wharton School of the University of Pennsylvania

材料学院教师在美国罗格斯大学电子和计算机工程系进行为期一个月的访学工作
Faculty of the School of Materials Science and Engineering attending a one-month program at the Department of Electrical and Computer Engineering of Rutgers University

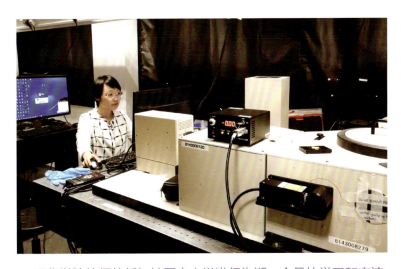

环化学院教师赴新加坡国立大学进行为期一个月的学习和交流
Faculty of the School of Environmental and Chemical Engineering attending a one-month program at the National University of Singapore

悉尼工商学院教师赴澳大利亚悉尼科技大学进行为期一个月的访学交流
Faculty of SILC attending a one-month program at UTS

美术学院中英合作天然染色时尚织物设计工作营
Sino-British Natural Dyeing Fashion Fabric Design Camp held by Shanghai Academy of Fine Arts at SHU

33名学生赴美国德克萨斯大学奥斯汀分校进行为期三周的专业学习
Thirty-three SHU students attending a three-week summer program at University of Texas at Austin

7个人文类学院的20名学生参加英国牛津大学和剑桥大学人文课程暑期项目
Students of SHU humanities programs attending a summer program at Oxford and Cambridge

美国纽约大学 IMPACT 暑期艺术实习项目
Students joining the IMPACT Summer Art Internship Program at New York University

美国迪士尼春季、秋季实习项目
The intern students joining Disney College Programs

中国对外友好合作服务中心海外专业实习项目
Students joining the overseas internship programs organized by China Service Center for Friendship and Cooperation with Foreign Countries

（四）孔子学院
Confucius Institutes

泰国宋卡王子大学普吉孔子学院学生文艺表演

Recreational activities at the Confucius Institute, Prince of Songkla University, Thailand

爱尔兰科克大学孔子学院课堂

Classroom teaching at the Confucius Institute, University College Cork, Ireland

2010年4月14日，中共中央政治局常委李长春、土耳其海峡大学校长卡迪里为上海大学与海峡大学共建的海峡大学孔子学院揭牌

Li Changchun, a member of the Standing Committee of the Political Bureau of the CPC Central Committee and Kadir, President of Boğaziçi Üniversitesi unveiling the Confucius Institute co-founded by Boğaziçi Üniversitesi and SHU, April 14, 2010

第三部分　1994年至今的上海大学　　　　　　　　　　　　　　　　　　　　　　八、国际交流与合作

2013年12月7日，国家汉办授予上海大学"孔子学院先进中方合作院校"称号，中共中央政治局委员、国务院副总理刘延东为上海大学授牌

Liu Yandong, Vice Premier of State Council, presenting the medal to SHU, winner of the "Outstanding Chinese Partner of Confucius Institute," December 7, 2013

2014年4月15日，上海大学与巴林大学共建的巴林大学孔子学院揭牌，上海市副市长翁铁慧出席

The unveiling ceremony of the Confucius Institute at Bahrain, co-founded by SHU and University of Bahrain, attended by Weng Tiehui, Vice Mayor of Shanghai, April 15, 2014,

2017年9月25日，校长金东寒率团参加美国肯塔基大学"全球示范孔院"揭牌仪式

President Jin Donghan attending the unveiling ceremony of the Global Model Confucius Institute at University of Kentucky, September 25, 2017

九

服务社会
Social Services

成人教育学院在2002、2007年两次被评为全国自学考试先进集体，2005、2006年两次被评为全国成人高等学校招生工作先进集体

The College of Continuing Education of SHU, winning the Award of National Outstanding Unit of Self-Study Examination in 2002 and 2007, and the Award of the National Outstanding Unit of Adult Higher Education Enrollment in 2005 and 2006

2005年成立上海市企业家培训基地

The founding of Shanghai Enterpreneurship Training Base, 2005

2007年12月17日，与云南大学签署对口支援两校合作协议

Cooperation agreement signing ceremony between SHU and Yunnan University, December17, 2007

2009年10月27日，举行"上海紧缺人才培训工程'纳米科技与应用能力'上海大学培训点"授牌仪式

The unveiling ceremony of SHU Training Center for Talents in Nanometer Technology and Application, part of Shanghai Training Project for Urgently-Needed Professionals, October 27, 2009

2015年6月，由文化部非遗司主办、上海大学上海美术学院承办的"中国非遗传承人群研培计划"试点工作现场协调会议在学校召开。2017年11月，"2017年中国非遗传承人群培计划经验交流会"及作品交流展在学校召开，集中呈现全国78所研培高校的教学成果和工作经验，文化部副部长项兆伦、文化部非遗司司长陈通出席

The coordination meeting of the pilot work of Research and Training Program for Talents of Chinese Intangible Cultural Heritage at SHU in June 2015. The Art Exhibition and the Experience Exchange Meeting of Talents Training for Intangible Cultural Heritage at SHU were held in November 2017, attended by Xiang Zhaolun, Vice Minister of Culture, and Chen Tong, Director of the Intangible Cultural Heritage Department of the Ministry of Culture.

2018年1月21日，校党委书记、校长金东寒与中国文化新经济开发标准研究委员会主任赵迪（左）为上海大学文化新经济研究院揭牌。该院已参与了苏州姑苏区等"国家文化新经济开发标准试验区"建设

The Institute of the New Economy Cultural Development, SHU, unveiled by President Jin Donghan and Zhao Di (left), Director of the Committee on Standardization of the Chinese New Cultural Economy, January 21, 2018

2018年5月，美术学院教师章莉莉获文化和旅游部颁发的"全国非物质文化遗产保护工作先进个人称号"

Zhang Lili, a teacher of the Academy of Fine Arts, awarded the title of "National Outstanding Individual in the Protection of Intangible Cultural Heritage" by the Ministry of Culture and Tourism, May 2018

2019年2月，美术学院教师苏金成主持的"荇村小讲堂"志愿服务项目获中央精神文明指导委员会颁发的宣传推广学雷锋志愿服务"四个100"最佳志愿服务项目

"Art Classes at Fengcun Village," a volunteer program organized by Su Jincheng, a teacher of the Academy of Fine Arts, awarded National Best Volunteer Service Project for the promotion of Lei Feng spirit by the Central Spiritual Civilization Steering Committee, February 2019

2020年7月13日，校党委常委、总会计师苟燕楠到延长校区科技园走访调研入驻企业

Gou Yannan, Chief Finance Officer of SHU, visiting the enterprises in the SHU Science and Technology Park on Yanchang Road, July 13, 2020

精神文明建设

Campus Activities

（一）全国文明校园和上海世博会先进集体
National Model Campus and Excellent Unit of Shanghai World Expo

2017年11月，获首届"全国文明校园"称号
SHU winning the title of the first National Model Campus, November 2017

2010年12月，校团委被中共中央、国务院授予"上海世博会先进集体"
The Youth League Committee of SHU was awarded the Excellent Unit of Shanghai World Expo by the CPC Central Committee and the State Council, December 2010.

（二）讲座　Lectures

2007—2011年，学校陆续出版《上大演讲录》系列丛书（7卷），收录知名学者到校演讲稿
Lectures of Shanghai University (7 volumes), a collection of full speech transcripts of notable scholars lecturing at SHU, published by Shanghai University Press from 2007 to 2011

原文化部部长王蒙到校演讲
Wang Meng, Minister of Culture from 1986 to 1989, giving a lecture at SHU

著名作家莫言到校演讲

Mo Yan, the 2012 Nobel Prize Winner in literature, giving a lecture at SHU

敦煌研究院名誉院长、"双百人物"樊锦诗研究员到校演讲

Fan Jinshi, a Chinese archaeologist and heritage specialist, honorary director and fellow of the Dunhuang Academy, giving a lecture at SHU

（三）国际大师讲坛
Masters' Seminars

诺贝尔物理学奖获得者安东尼·莱格特教授到校演讲

Anthony J. Leggett, the 2003 Nobel Prize Winner in physics, giving a lecture at SHU

美国工程院院士，宾夕法尼亚大学大卫·斯洛洛维茨教授到校演讲

David J. Srolovitz, a professor of University of Pennsylvania and academician of American Academy of Engineering, giving a lecture at SHU

诺贝尔物理学奖获得者迈克尔·科斯特利茨教授到校演讲
J. Michael Kosterlitz, the 2016 Nobel Prize Winner in physics, giving a lecture at SHU

诺贝尔化学奖获得者卡尔·巴里·夏普莱斯教授到校演讲
Karl Barry Sharpless, the 2001 Nobel Prize Winner in chemistry, giving a lecture at SHU

诺贝尔物理学奖获得者克劳斯·冯·克利钦教授到校演讲
Klaus von Klitzing, the 1985 Nobel Prize Winner in physics, giving a lecture at SHU

（四）文体活动
Recreational Activities

2004年9月1日，承办第七届全国大学生运动会
The 7th National University Games hosted by SHU, September 1, 2004

2007年11月5日，承办上海市首届科教工作者运动会
The 1st Sports Meeting of the Staff Working with Science and Education hosted by SHU, November 5, 2007

2007年12月27日，举办2008年中外学生迎新年联欢晚会
The 2008 SHU Chinese and International Students' New Year Party, December 27, 2007

从2005年起，学校每年举办"泮池之声"新年音乐会。图为由著名指挥家曹鹏指挥的2011年新年音乐会
Cao Peng conducting the SHU Annual New Year Concert, January 7, 2011

（五）校园文化
Campus Culture

研究生学术节着重营造学术氛围，提升学术热情与能力，在传承中引导锐意创新、严谨踏实的学术精神

The annual Academic Festival of Graduate Students, enhancing the academic enthusiasm and creativity and building the truth-seeking spirit for the budding researchers

研究生艺术节着重优化研究生的审美能力，在中华优秀传统文化教育的熏陶下能够欣赏、感悟文化之美

The annual Art Festival of Graduate Students, cultivating students' aesthetic sense and creativity

研究生体育节着重培养研究生的锻炼习惯，在不断开拓创新的过程中，具备良好的心理和身体素质

The annual Sports Festival of Graduate Students, strengthening the body and soul

菊文化节始于 2003 年，至 2019 年已举办十七届。图为 2019 年第十七届菊文化节

The 17th Annual Chrysanthemum Culture Festival of SHU, 2019

2017 年 7 月 6 日，举办百变巾帼喜迎十九大——上海大学第二届女教职工服饰展演

The 2nd Fashion Show of Female Faculty at SHU, July 6, 2017

社团文化节始于 2011 年，至 2019 年已举办九届。图为 2019 年 4 月 17 日举办的第九届社团文化节

The 9th Festival of SHU Societies, April 17, 2019

国际文化节始于 2007 年，至 2019 年已举办七届。图为 2019 年 5 月 9 日举办的第七届国际文化节开幕式

The opening ceremony of the 7th International Festival & Custom Exhibition, May 9, 2019

第三部分　1994年至今的上海大学　　　　　　　　　　　　　　　　　　　十、精神文明建设

2014年10月23日，上海大学（1922-1927）纪念园——溯园开放
Suyuan, the SHU (1922-1927) Memorial Garden

2016年12月17日，举办第十五届海派文化学术研讨会
The 15th Seminar on Haipai (Shanghai School) Culture at SHU, December 17, 2016

2019年12月19日，召开全国红色文化战略联盟成立大会，来自全国18个省、市、自治区的高等院校、红色纪念场馆和企业党建的近百名代表参加会议
The founding conference of the National Red Culture Alliance at SHU, attended by nearly 100 representatives from universities, museums, and enterprises nationwide, December 19, 2019

（六）应征入伍，捐献造血干细胞
Joining the Army and Donating Stem Cells

2006年12月23日，召开冬季征兵欢送大会
The farewell ceremony held for SHU non-graduates recruited in PLA, December 23, 2006

2002年6月，法学院孙晓磊为一名浙江患儿成功捐献造血干细胞，成为上海大学第一例、上海市第10例捐献者。从2012年6月至2019年，学校共有12名学生成功捐献骨髓

Sun Xiaolei, a student of the Law School, successfully donated hematopoietic stem cells to a child patient from Zhejiang in June 2002. Sun is the 1st stem cell donor at SHU and the 10th in Shanghai. A total of 12 volunteers from SHU have donated bone marrow from June 2012 to 2019.

01 法学院 — 孙晓磊　Sun Xiaolei, the Law School
02 机自学院 — 黄亮　Huang Liang, the School of Mechatronic Engineering and Automation
03 生命学院 — 倪继祖　Ni Jizu, the School of Life Sciences
04 法学院 — 葛菁　Ge Jing, the Law School
05 法学院 — 高薇　Gao Wei, the Law School
06 文学院 — 雷秋琴　Lei Qiuqin, the College of Liberal Arts
07 中欧学院 — 郑钦文　Zheng Qinwen, the Sino-European School of Technology
08 生命学院 — 左祎　Zuo Yi, the School of Life Sciences
09 通信学院 — 周欢　Zhou Huan, the School of Communication & Information Engineering
10 环化学院 — 窦大营　Dou Daying, the School of Environmental and Chemical Engineering
11 通信学院 — 孙闯　Sun Chuang, the School of Communication & Information Engineering
12 电影学院 — 王昊　Wang Hao, the Shanghai Film Academy

（七）志愿者服务
Volunteering Services

自 2003 年起，学校累计派遣 164 名学生参加大学生志愿服务西部计划。图为学校学生参加 2007 年 7 月 20 日举行的上海市大学生志愿服务西部计划出征仪式暨表彰大会
Students of SHU attending the departure and award ceremony for "Go West" Volunteer Program (Shanghai), July 20, 2007

2010 年 12 月，校团委被中共中央、国务院授予"上海世博会先进集体"。图为学校举行世博会志愿者誓师动员大会
The SHU World Expo Volunteer Mobilization Meeting, June 21, 2010. In December, The Youth League Committee of SHU was awarded the Excellent Unit of Shanghai World Expo by the CPC Central Committee and the State Council, December 2010.

2018 年 11 月，参加首届中国国际进口博览会的志愿者
Volunteers from SHU serving the 1st China International Import Expo, November 2018

（八）疫情防控
Epidemic Prevention and Control

2020年2月27日，上海市教卫工作党委书记沈炜到延长校区实地调研新冠肺炎疫情防控工作，校党委书记成旦红、校长刘昌胜、校党委副书记欧阳华、副校长聂清陪同调研

Shen Wei, Secretary of the CPC Committee of Shanghai Municipal Education and Health Work, visiting SHU during the COVID-19 pandemic, accompanied by Secretary of the Party Committee of SHU Cheng Danhong, President Liu Changsheng, Deputy Secretary Ouyang Hua, and Vice President Nie Qing, February 27, 2020

2020年4月26日，学校组织开展疫情防控应急处置演练

The emergency response drill for the prevention and control of the pandemic, April 26, 2020

十一

校友工作
Alumni Activities

（一）情系母校
Supports from the Alumni

2020年7月3日，上海大学2020届毕业典礼当晚，19：22-20：20（寓意从1922—2020年），上海中心大厦为毕业生送上来自云端的祝福。自2016年起，中国第一、世界第二高楼的上海中心大厦每年为上海大学毕业生亮灯，活动得到了校友们的大力支持

On the evening of the graduation ceremony of SHU for the Class of 2020, July 3, 2020, best wishes to the graduates were sent from the Shanghai Tower, the tallest building in China and the second tallest in the world, from 19:22 to 20:20, indicating a centennial history of SHU from 1922 to 2020. This event started from 2016 and is funded by SHU alumni.

2018年1月，党委书记、校长金东寒为支持母校建设的彭宏陵校友颁发卓越贡献奖

President Jin Donghan presenting Outstanding Contribution Award to Peng Hongling for his consistent supports for the development of SHU, January 2018

2018年1月，校党委书记、校长金东寒，党委副书记徐旭为上海新航星投资集团有限公司董事长、上海大学校董、校友会副会长何志明颁发捐赠证书

President Jin Donghan and Deputy Secretary of the Party Committee Xu Xu presenting the donation certificate to He Zhiming, Chairman of the Board of Shanghai New Sail Star Group, January 2018

2018年8月，上海大学校董、校友会副会长周忻和校友会副会长朱旭东联合创立的易居（中国）控股有限公司签约捐赠5000万元设立易居校长基金

The Easyhouse President's Fund was established in August 2018. Easyhouse (China) Holding Co., LTD, co-founded by Zhou Xin, trustee of SHU and Vice Chairman of the SHU Alumni Association, and Zhu Xudong, Vice Chairman of the SHU Alumni Association, donated 50 million yuan to the fund.

2019年10月11日，上海大学（原上海工业大学）1979级研究生入学40周年纪念会举行。校长刘昌胜、校党委副书记欧阳华接待校友

The former graduate students of SHU (formerly SUT) coming back to celebrate the 40th anniversary of the admission in 1979, received by President Liu Changsheng and Deputy Secretary of the Party Committee Ouyang Hua, October 11, 2019

（二）校友会
Alumni Associations

2016年4月28日，来华留学生校友分会成立
The founding ceremony of the International Alumni Association, April 28, 2016

2016年6月3日，英国校友会成立大会在英国伦敦举行
The founding ceremony of Britain Branch of Alumni Association in London, UK, June 3, 2016

2018年3月31日，日本校友会成立大会在日本东京举行
The founding ceremony of Japan Branch of Alumni Association in Tokyo, Japan, March 31, 2018

2018年12月22日，北京校友会成立
The founding ceremony of Beijing Branch of Alumni Association, December 22, 2018

2019年7月20日，首家行业校友会"人工智能行业校友会"成立
The founding ceremony of SHU Alumni Association of Artificial Intelligence, the first industry alumni association, July 20, 2019

2019年9月26日，泰国校友会在泰国普吉成立
The founding ceremony of Thailand Branch of Alumni Association in Phuket, Thailand, September 26, 2019

2019年9月29日，加拿大校友会在加拿大多伦多成立
The founding ceremony of Canada Branch of Alumni Association in Toronto, Canada, September 29, 2019

Current leaders of Shanghai University

百年上大，世代情缘

SHU Memories, Passing Down Generations

从 1922 年到 2020 年，从老上大到新上大，邓果白、邓伟志、邓瞳瞳，郭毅、郭健、郭亮、郭唯博，跨越世纪的历史偶遇，隐喻着上大薪火代代相传。

SHU has become the tradition of the Deng Famliy and the Guo Family. Grandparents, parents, children and grandchildren attended and worked at SHU successively in the centennial history of SHU from 1922 to 2020, passing down the spirit and memories of SHU from generation to generation.

邓果白（1907—1967），1925年秋进入上海大学学习
Deng Guobai (1907-1967) entered SHU in 1925.

邓伟志（1938— ），邓果白儿子，上海大学终身教授，第九届、第十届全国政协常委
Deng Weizhi (1938-), Deng Guobai's son, a tenured professor of SHU and member of the Standing Committee of the Ninth and Tenth CPPCC National Committee

邓瞳瞳（1969— ），邓伟志女儿，1987—1991年就读于上海大学社会学系
Deng Tongtong (1969-), Deng Weizhi's daughter, studied at the Sociology Department of SHU from 1987 to 1991.

郭毅（1905—1942），又名郭君毅，1924年进入上海大学社会学系学习

Guo Yi (1905-1942) studied at the Sociology Department of SHU from 1924.

郭健（1931— ），郭毅侄子，1988年2月—1989年7月在上海大学文学院行政管理专业高等教育专业证书班学习

Guo Jian (1931-), Guo Yi's nephew, attending a non-degree program at the College of Liberal Arts of SHU from February 1988 to July 1989

郭亮（1963— ），郭健女儿，1985年至今在上海大学工作

Guo Liang (1963-), Guo Jian's daughter, working at SHU from 1985

郭唯博（1982— ），郭毅重孙，2001—2005年就读于上海大学材料科学与工程学院

Guo Weibo (1982-), great grandson of Guo Yi, attending the School of Materials Science and Engineering of SHU from 2001 to 2005

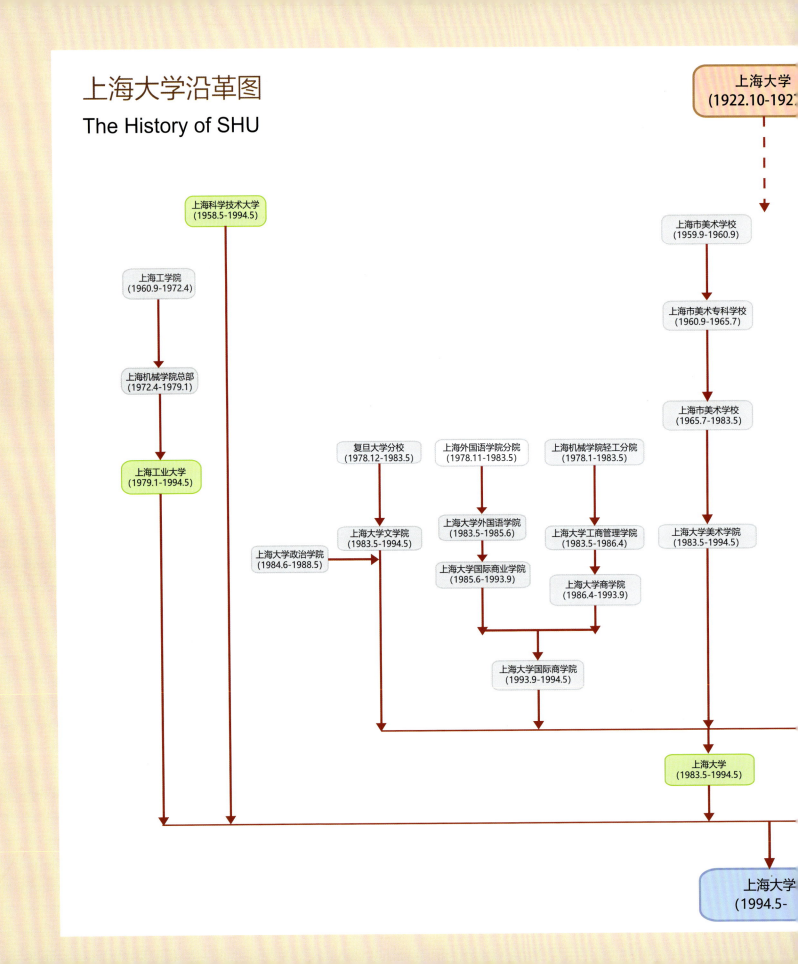

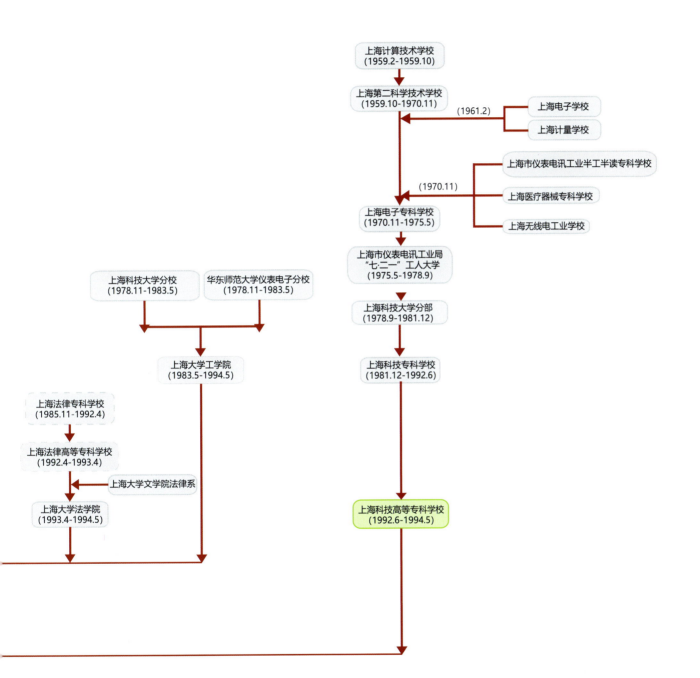

图书在版编目（CIP）数据

百年上大画传 / 成旦红，刘昌胜主编 .—上海：上海大学出版社，
2020.9（2020.10 重印）
 ISBN 978-7-5671-3918-3

Ⅰ. ①百… Ⅱ. ①成… ②刘… Ⅲ. ①上海大学—校史—图集
Ⅳ. ① G649.285.1-64

中国版本图书馆 CIP 数据核字（2020）第 142376 号

责任编辑　傅玉芳　刘　强　石伟丽
　　　　　陈　强　王悦生　祝艺菲
技术编辑　金　鑫　钱宇坤
装帧设计　柯国富

百年上大画传

成旦红　刘昌胜　主编

出版发行	上海大学出版社
社　　址	上海市上大路99号
邮政编码	200444
网　　址	www.shupress.cn
发行热线	021-66135112
出 版 人	戴骏豪
印　　刷	上海颛辉印刷厂有限公司
经　　销	各地新华书店
开　　本	889mm×1194mm 1/12
印　　张	28
字　　数	560千字
版　　次	2020年9月第1版
印　　次	2020年10月第2次
书　　号	ISBN 978-7-5671-3918-3/G・3132
定　　价	320.00元